If You Need to Slow the Hell Down Was a Person
Person
The Case of the Missing Luggage

If You Need to Slow the Hell Down Was a Person

Person

The Case of the Missing Luggage
by Chanel Brooks
Brooks Empowerment Publishing

Published by
Brooks Empowerment Publishing
www.ChanelBrooks.com
ISBN: 979-8-9952515-0-7
Cover design by Chanel B. Brooks
Interior design by Brooks Empowerment Publishing
Printed in the United States of America

First Edition

Dedication

To the Mighty God,

My source, my covering, my constant.

Every step of this journey was guided by Your hand, even when I didn't realize it at the time.

To my mother, Patricia Edwards,

Thank you for giving me the blueprint on how to be strong, resilient, and rooted.

You have been my forever ride-or-die, my safe place, my example of grace under pressure, and my greatest blessing. Everything I am is because of you.

To my stepfather, Ronald Edwards,

Thank you for loving my mom the way that you do.

To my husband, Donoven Ray Brooks,

Thank you for loving me through every version of me—the strong one, the stubborn one, the "I've got it handled" one, and the one who finally admitted she didn't have to handle everything alone.

You taught me something I had spent years forgetting: that partnership means I don't have to carry the weight of the world by myself.

Thank you for your patience, your steadiness, and for giving me the safe space to finally unpack my luggage.

And because of you, I now know what it feels like to live in my full femininity—supported, loved, and at peace.

To my son, Jordan Reed—my purpose,

Son, you will never fully know how much of who I am exists because of you.

Because of you, I AM.

I love you to the moon and back, and I am endlessly proud of the young man you are becoming.

To my brothers, Andre, Maurice, and Lafayette,

My guardians and protectors from my inception—thank you for always standing watch, always having my back, and always reminding me that I was never alone.

To my bonus children—Jaden, Kai, Cherell, and Don, Jr.,

Thank you for allowing me into your lives and hearts. Loving you has expanded my world in the most beautiful way.

To my sister-in-law, Lynn Wall,

You had no idea that your presence, your words, and your example would be the final push I needed to complete this book—but it was. Thank you for walking in purpose and unknowingly helping me step fully into mine.

To my supporters, my besties, and yes—even my haters,

Thank you. Every cheer, every challenge, every doubt helped sharpen my voice and strengthen my resolve.

To my Sistahs in Transformation,

Thank you for being my circle of healing, growth, truth, and sisterhood.

You held space for me in every season and reminded me that this work—this becoming—is not meant to be done alone.

A special thank you to Kenya Purnell.

You had no idea that a simple phone call would become a defining moment in this journey. When you called to tell me I had left my luggage behind—and helped coordinate its safe return—you unknowingly gave me the metaphor that named this entire book.

That moment became clarity.

That call became confirmation.

That "missing luggage" became the language for everything women carry, forget, lose, and must intentionally reclaim.

Sometimes the Universe uses the smallest interruptions to deliver the biggest revelations.

And finally, to my readers—

Thank you for choosing this book. I hope you find the gems within these pages helpful and applicable to your own life. My prayer is that this book helps guide you to your own soft space.

Because sis… you don't know it yet, but you are HER.

With love and gratitude,

Chanel Brooks

Table of Contents

Choosing peace, balance, and joy after the hard work of healing.

Final Chapter
She Rises: Stepping Into the Rest of Your Life
(Where Survival Ends and Sovereignty Begins)
The moment you realize your life belongs to you again.

Book Club Discussion Guide
Reflection Questions & Healing Exercises

Foreword

There comes a moment in life when the pace we have been keeping suddenly feels unsustainable.

The endless responsibilities.

The constant expectations.

The silent pressure to keep showing up for everyone else. For many women, especially those who are strong, capable, and dependable, slowing down can feel almost impossible. We have been conditioned to believe that success means doing more, giving more, sacrificing more. And somewhere along the way, we learn to carry the weight of everyone else's needs while quietly placing our own at the bottom of the list. Until one day we realize something has to change.

If You Need to Slow the Hell Down Was a Person: The Case of the Missing Luggage is not just a book. It is a wake-up call. A reminder that the life you deserve cannot be lived at a pace that leaves you exhausted, overwhelmed, and disconnected from yourself.

In these pages, Chanel B. Brooks invites you to pause and reflect on the patterns many of us fall into without even realizing it. With honesty, insight, and a refreshing dose of humor, she challenges the belief that being everything for everyone else is the ultimate measure of success.

Instead, she offers something far more powerful: permission.

Permission to breathe.

Permission to rest.

Permission to set boundaries.

Permission to choose yourself again.

This book reminds us that slowing down is not weakness. It is wisdom. It is clarity. It is the moment when we reclaim our time, our energy, and our lives.

If you have ever felt stretched too thin, pulled in too many directions, or unsure how to step off the relentless treadmill of expectations, this book will speak directly to you.

Let these words serve as your invitation to rediscover balance, redefine success, and remember that your well-being matters just as much as everything else you have been holding together.
The journey begins the moment you decide that your peace is worth protecting.
And that moment can begin right now.

If You Need to Slow the Hell Down Was a Person
Person
The Case of the Missing Luggage
by Chanel Brooks

What happens when a woman stops surviving… and starts living?

In If Slow the Hell Down Was a Person, Chanel Brooks delivers a bold, soul-stirring guide for women who are tired of hustling through life, carrying emotional luggage that no longer fits, and waiting for permission to rest, rise, and receive.

This is not a book about pretending everything is fine.

It's about healing in real time.

Through personal storytelling, cultural insight, and practical frameworks like the D.A.M.N. Method (Digest, Accept, Move, Note-take), Chanel invites readers to release survival mode, reclaim their identity, and step fully into alignment, softness, and self-worth.

From navigating burnout and reinvention, to finding love later in life, setting unshakable boundaries, and choosing peace without guilt—this book meets women exactly where they are and gently guides them forward.

You won't find clichés or empty motivation here.

You'll find truth. Wisdom. And permission.

Because slowing down isn't quitting—

it's choosing yourself.

And sometimes, the life you prayed for arrives only after you finally put the luggage down.

From One "HER to Another!

Chanel Brooks

Chapter One

✦ The Case of the Missing Luggage

(The Universe's Way of Saying: "Not So Fast, Sis")

INTRODUCTION: A BEGINNING MEANT TO SHAKE YOU AWAKE

I knew I needed that weekend more than I admitted.

You know how you tell people you're "just tired," but deep down you're not tired — you're depleted? That was me. I was functioning. Performing, even. I was showing up everywhere I was expected to be, smiling in all the right places, answering texts, returning calls, handling responsibilities, solving problems, being dependable. I had become extremely good at being the person everyone could count on.

What I wasn't good at anymore... was hearing myself.

So when the invitation came for a girls' retreat with my Sistahs in Transformation family at The Mansion on Noble Lane, I didn't hesitate. My body said yes before my mind could start negotiating all the reasons I should stay home and "handle things."
Because women like me always have things to handle.
I packed like a woman preparing to be responsible for herself and three other people — even though nobody asked me to.
I packed options.
I packed backups.
I packed a "just in case."
I packed an outfit in case I didn't like the first outfit.
And I definitely packed shoes that had no business being worn at a peaceful retreat but made me feel prepared for a life emergency that was not scheduled to happen.
Packing, for me, has never been just packing. It's control.
If I'm prepared, I'm safe.
If I'm organized, nothing can fall apart.
If I've planned enough, life won't catch me off guard.
Or at least that's what I had convinced myself.

The Retreat

The mansion was beautiful in the kind of way that forces you to slow down whether you want to or not. Trees surrounded the property like they had been guarding peace there long before we arrived. The air felt quieter. Even the sunlight seemed calmer.
We weren't rushing to meetings.
We weren't answering work emails.
Nobody needed anything from us.
And for the first time in a long time, I noticed how strange that felt.
We laughed — real laughter, the kind that comes from your stomach and not your social mask. We played games and argued over rules like kids again. We sat around sharing stories we usually only hint at in passing conversations. We got facials, massages,

walked in silence, and let ourselves be still long enough for our thoughts to finally catch up to us.

I didn't realize how loud my life had been until I heard quiet.

The first night, I slept deeply — not exhausted sleep, but peaceful sleep. The kind where your shoulders finally unclench without you noticing.

By the second day, my breathing slowed. I wasn't checking my phone every ten minutes. I wasn't mentally planning next week while standing in the present moment.

I was there.

And that sounds simple, but for women who carry everything for everyone, being present is unfamiliar territory.

By Sunday morning, something in me had softened. Not weakened — softened. There's a difference. I felt lighter without anything in my life actually changing yet.

We took pictures before leaving, hugging, promising not to let so much time pass before doing this again. You know those conversations women have when we're sincere in the moment, but life often swallows our intentions afterward.

I loaded my car, said my final goodbyes, and drove away feeling full.

I thought I was leaving with memories.

I didn't realize I had left with a lesson.

The Drive

The drive home was about three hours. I had music playing softly and the kind of peaceful silence that only comes when your mind isn't racing ahead of you.

But slowly, as the miles passed, real life began re-entering my thoughts.

The responsibilities waiting.

The calls I needed to return.

The roles I stepped back into the moment I arrived home.

I could feel myself mentally picking everything back up —
schedules, expectations, emotional labor — like coats hanging by a
door I was about to walk back through.
Women don't clock out of their lives. We pause them.
And I was preparing to resume mine.
About two and a half hours into the drive, my phone rang.
I answered casually, expecting a "Did you make it home yet?"
check-in.
Instead, I heard:
"Hey sis… um… you missing something?"
I laughed lightly. "No, I don't think so."
A pause.
"Your orange suitcase is still here."
Silence.
Not outside the car — inside me.
My brain tried to process what she said and immediately rejected it.
"No it's not," I replied automatically.
Because I don't forget things.
I am the reminder person. The double-checker. The "Did
everybody bring their charger?" friend. The one who notices
details.
Except this time… I hadn't.
I had driven almost three hours.
Without my suitcase.

The Moment
I pulled the car over.
Not because I needed directions.
Because I needed a minute.
I laughed first — the polite laugh we use when our brain hasn't
caught up to our emotions yet.
Then came the realization.
I didn't just leave my suitcase.
I never even noticed it was gone.

Not when I said goodbye.
Not when I loaded the car.
Not when I started driving.
Not for almost three hours.
I sat there staring ahead, hands on the steering wheel, and a strange
thought crossed my mind:
**How disconnected from myself had I been that I could leave
something behind and not even feel its absence?**
That suitcase held my clothes, yes.
But more than that, it represented preparation, control, readiness
— the version of me that keeps everything together at all times.
And yet… without it, nothing catastrophic had happened.
I was still okay.
I wasn't stranded.
I wasn't incapable.
I wasn't falling apart.
I was… fine.
Actually, I was more peaceful than I'd felt in a long time.
And that's when it hit me.

The Realization

For years I had been carrying responsibilities, expectations,
emotional burdens, and roles so automatically that I no longer
noticed their weight.
I had learned to function inside pressure so well that I thought
constant motion was normal.
I thought exhaustion was adulthood.
I thought overextending was love.
I thought being needed was the same as being fulfilled.
But sitting there on the side of the road, realizing I had traveled
almost the entire distance home without noticing my luggage was
missing, I understood something quietly but clearly:
I had been moving through my life the same way.
Present physically.

Absent emotionally.
Managing everything.
Experiencing very little.
The suitcase wasn't a crisis.
It was a mirror.
I hadn't just forgotten luggage.
I had forgotten to notice myself.
And maybe — just maybe — the pause I experienced that weekend wasn't meant to stay at the retreat. Maybe it was meant to follow me home and show me that I could put things down and still be whole.
I turned the car back onto the road, lighter than I had any reason to be.
Because for the first time, I wondered:
If I could survive a weekend without controlling everything…
what else in my life was I carrying that I no longer needed to?
That question — not the suitcase — is where this story truly begins.

We Carry Too Much—And Nobody Teaches Us to Put It Down

Women are conditioned to carry:

- Homes
- Families
- Emotional labor
- Unpaid labor
- The weight of everyone's expectations
- Trauma we never asked for
- Responsibilities we never volunteered for

And somewhere between being everything to everyone and nothing to ourselves, we forget who we are.
"Sometimes God removes what you packed so He can return what you need."

This chapter is your reminder — your soft landing and your stern wake-up call — that you cannot pour from an empty cup. You can't sprint through life and expect peace to catch up to you. You cannot keep showing up for the world while abandoning yourself in the process.

The True Message Behind the Missing Suitcase

That moment became a symbol — a loud, neon, divine symbol — of what so many of us women refuse to acknowledge:

- We are exhausted from carrying bags that don't belong to us.
- We are burdened by responsibilities that no longer serve us.
- We are speeding through experiences we should be savoring.
- We are living, but not always present.
- We are giving, but not always receiving.
- We are strong — but sometimes too strong for our own good.

"You can't smell the roses if you're always running past the garden."

The missing suitcase taught me:

✓ I needed to slow down even more.

✓ I wasn't as present as I thought.

✓ I was still clutching the old version of me out of habit.

✓ And I had to let go of the weight — physical, emotional, spiritual — that was slowing me down.

The truth is, I didn't need anything inside that suitcase in that moment.

Everything I needed was already in me — restored, refreshed, renewed.

"A woman becomes unstoppable the moment she realizes she already possesses what she was searching for."

Even celebrity women—women with money, glam teams, chefs, and assistants—speak about this openly.

✦ **Gabrielle Union** once shared that she carried childhood trauma into her career, marriage, and motherhood because she was always in "fix-it mode."

✦ **Michelle Obama** admitted she lost herself while being everything to everyone, and had to rewrite her identity.

✦ **Mary J. Blige** has said she spent years performing strength until she learned to allow softness.

These are women with resources—yet they STILL carried too much.

So what does that mean for the everyday woman who's juggling life without a staff?

It means we push past exhaustion like it's normal.

It means we collapse silently because we were never allowed to sit loudly.

Let this land:

"Sometimes God removes what you packed so He can return what you ACTUALLY need."

"When a woman chooses herself, the world feels the shift."

✦ You shine brighter.

✦ You breathe deeper.

✦ Your boundaries sharpen.

✦ Your spirit rises.

✦ Your energy settles into its rightful throne.

✦ Your joy returns home to you.

✦ Your power moves differently.

✦ Your future expands instantly.

✦ And every room you walk into becomes aware…

that HER has arrived."

Celebrity Parallel: BEYONCÉ + The Suitcase Moment

Even **Beyoncé**—the hardest-working woman in entertainment—hit her suitcase moment.

During her "Homecoming" documentary, she admitted she was overworked, overwhelmed, and disconnected from her body and soul.

She had to stop.

Say no.

Rebuild.

Rest.

Create boundaries.

If Beyoncé can forget herself in the grind…

Sis, so can you.

Real Women. Real Breakdowns. Real Breakthroughs.

When I began sharing my story, other women started sharing theirs:

❤ A nurse who forgot her own birthday because she worked 16-hour shifts

❤ A mother who drove to daycare only to realize her child was already at school

❤ A CEO who left her laptop at TSA because she hadn't slept in two days

These weren't "mistakes."

They were *messages*.

Women don't fall apart when we're weak.

We fall apart when we've been too strong for too long.

Let this land:

"You can't smell the roses if you're sprinting past the garden."

When The Universe Get Petty With Your Growth

(And You Can't Even Be Mad About It)

Sis… let's talk about the moments when the Universe shows its sense of humor.

Because sometimes the Universe doesn't whisper.

It doesn't nudge.

It doesn't gently encourage growth.

No.

Sometimes the Universe gets just a *little* petty with the way it pushes you into alignment.

Not to harm you —

but to remind you who you are

and to force you toward who you're becoming.

Here are the classic signs:

The Universe Will Snatch Something You Weren't Brave Enough to Put Down

You say you're done.

You swear you're done.

You tell your girls you're done.

But you're *not* done.

So the Universe steps in like:

"Let me help you out, because clearly you're struggling."

The phone stops ringing.

They reveal who they really are.

The job cuts ties.

The friend exposes their jealousy.

And you're sitting there like:

"Wow. That was unnecessary."
The Universe:
"No, baby — that was alignment."

The Universe Will Let the Red Flags Tap Dance in Front of You

You ask for a sign…
and the Universe gives you a whole Broadway performance.
He lies.
He gaslights.
He ghosts.
He fumbles you publicly.
He acts like a man who has never heard of therapy.
And you're still like:
"Maybe he's just stressed."
The Universe:
"STRESSED? STRESSED?! Open your eyes, Sis."
When the Universe gets petty, it makes the truth loud enough to embarrass you into healing.

The Universe Will Give You a Blessing… Then Test If You're Ready to Keep It

You ask for peace.
The Universe gives it to you.
Then it sends:
- the ex
- the friend who drains you
- the coworker who thinks you're the office therapist
- the opportunity that looks good but isn't aligned

And the Universe stands back like:
"Let me see if she learned her boundaries."

If you fail, it'll run the test again…
and again…
and AGAIN.
Petty?
Absolutely.
Necessary?
Also yes.

The Universe Will Let Your "Almost" Fall Apart So Your "Absolutely" Can Find You

You're crying over a "situationship" the Universe never approved of.
You're grieving a relationship it blocked years ago.
You're mourning the future it never assigned to you.
Then you meet the partner the Universe actually sent for you and you're like:
"Wow. I was really out here begging for scraps."
The Universe:
"I TOLD YOU."
Divine pettiness: activated.
Divine timing: secured.

The Universe Will Not Let You Stay Where You Don't Belong — Even If You Want To

You're comfortable.
You're loyal.
You're committed.
You're invested.
But you've outgrown the situation.
So the Universe:

- closes the door
- makes the environment uncomfortable

- exposes the truth
- removes the mask
- interrupts your plans

And suddenly you're packing your emotional bags.

The Universe:

"I said what I said."

The Universe Will Elevate You Right in Front of the People Who Counted You Out

Your glow-up becomes their lesson.

Nothing humbles doubters faster than watching your blessings unfold like:

- promotions
- peace
- boundaries
- healthy love
- self-worth
- the soft life

And you don't have to do anything but exist.

The Universe:

"Try me again."

The Universe Will Make You Sit Still Until You Learn the Lesson

You're rushing.

Forcing.

Pushing.

Trying to make something happen.

The Universe hits you with delays:

- missed flights
- cancelled plans

- slow-moving progress
- unanswered calls
- silence

It feels petty…
but it's protection.
The Universe:
"If I let this happen now, it will destroy you later. TRUST ME."

The Petty Has Purpose

The Universe isn't petty to embarrass you.
It's petty to save you from:
- heartbreak
- stagnation
- misalignment
- trauma
- detours
- unnecessary suffering

Its pettiness is strategic.
Intentional.
Divinely calculated.
Its pettiness is your protection.
Its pettiness is your preparation.
Its pettiness is your PROMOTION.

A New Journey Begins

This book — this journey we're about to walk together — is your invitation to:

- Slow down
- Exhale
- Show up for yourself
- Release what you've been carrying

🌷 Reclaim your worth

🌷 And step boldly into the version of you that you forgot existed

Because hear me clearly:

Sis… YOU. ARE. HER.

You just have to remember.

So buckle up — and unpack.

Not just your suitcase, but your spirit.

Because if I can leave an orange suitcase three hours away and still find peace, joy, clarity, and purpose on the ride home…

Then baby, I promise you this:

By the end of this book, you're going to unpack things you didn't even know you were carrying — and you're going to step into the woman you were always meant to be.

"When the Universe gets petty, it's not punishment — it's elevation disguised as inconvenience." – Chanel Brooks

---

REFLECTION QUESTIONS FOR THE READER

Sit with these. Write if you can.

1.   **What have you been carrying that no longer belongs to you?**

2.   **What emotional "bags" do you keep repacking out of habit?**

3.   **Where in your life are you rushing past yourself?**

4.   **When was the last time you truly rested—not just slept?**

5.   **Who benefits from your exhaustion? Because it's not you.**

MINI-EXERCISE: "EMPTY THE SUITCASE"

Take a sheet of paper and draw a suitcase.

Inside it, write everything you're carrying that weighs you down:

•   Expectations

- Guilt
- Fear
- Burdens
- Responsibilities that are not yours
- Old stories
- Old battles

Then next to it, draw another suitcase:

Fill THIS one with:

- Peace
- Joy
- Boundaries
- Confidence
- Grace
- Permission to rest
- Permission to be human

This is your shift in visual form.

A New Journey Begins

This book is not entertainment.

It is transformation.

A roadmap.

A mirror.

A reset button.

Because Sis… let me say this clearly:

You're not lost.

You're just carrying too much.

And this is the moment you put it down.**

You are not entering a new chapter.

You are entering a new identity.

The woman you prayed to become?

YOU ARE HER.

This journey is about remembering.

So buckle up.

Unpack.

Let go.

And prepare for softness, clarity, and rebirth.

Because if I can leave an orange suitcase three hours away…

and still return home lighter than ever…

Baby, imagine what YOU'RE about to release.

Chapter Two
✦ Slow the Hell Down!
(The D.A.M.N. Method)

INTRODUCTION: WHEN SURVIVAL MODE BECOMES YOUR ADDRESS USED THE D.A.M.N. METHOD

Survival mode isn't loud.

It doesn't kick down the door or announce itself with warning lights.

Survival mode creeps in quietly.

It starts with a weary "I'm fine."

A forced smile.

A calendar full of responsibilities but an empty emotional tank.

It feels like:

- Making miracles out of nothing
- Carrying burdens quietly

- Swallowing feelings because there's "no time for breakdowns"
- Being everything to everyone while disappearing from yourself

And here's the dangerous truth:

If you stay in survival mode long enough, it starts to feel like home.

You stop believing in rest.

You stop expecting support.

You stop trusting joy.

You stop dreaming because you're too busy trying not to drown.

Many women — especially high-achievers, especially Black women — have lived so long in fight-or-flight that we confuse adrenaline with purpose.

Sis, hear this clearly:

You were never meant to live your entire life in emergency mode.

Section One: The Night Everything Collapsed (And Everything Shifted)

September 2006.

There are moments that change a woman — not softly, but suddenly.

This was one of those moments.

I didn't slide into rock bottom… I *collapsed* into it.

I laid across my bed in the dark, fully clothed, unable to muster the strength to pull a blanket over my body. This wasn't tired — this was *soul exhaustion*. The kind that whispers, "I don't know how to keep doing this."

My mind was spinning:

- The mortgage was late
- Daycare was due
- My gas tank was one mile from empty
- My credit cards were screaming
- My pride was heavy

- My options were gone

And my bank account?

It wasn't low.

It was *hollow.*

I wasn't living paycheck to paycheck.

I was living on fumes, fear, and whatever faith I had left.

So I cried.

Not the cute cry.

Not the TV cry.

I cried the cry of a woman who has held too much for too long.

The kind that shakes your chest and empties your spirit.

And when I had nothing left, I prayed.

Not eloquently.

Not elegantly.

Just… honestly.

"Lord… help me. I can't carry this alone anymore."

I didn't know that prayer had already been answered.

The Shift I Didn't See Coming

The next morning my phone rang.

My realtor's voice sounded almost cheerful:

"Chanel, he signed the papers. The house can move forward with the sale."

I sat up slowly.

I didn't scream.

I didn't rejoice.

I didn't dance.

I sat still — breathing a breath I hadn't felt in months.

Because sometimes miracles don't enter loudly…

Sometimes they glide in quietly and simply whisper:

"See? You weren't forgotten."

Something shifted in me that morning.
Not because life was suddenly perfect — it wasn't.
But because I realized something crucial:
I had survived what should have broken me.
And I was tired of living like my life was one long emergency.

Celebrity Parallels: Even Powerful Women Break Down

You are not alone.
Even the strongest women — the ones we admire, the ones who look invincible — have faced their own "September 2006" moments.

 Taraji P. Henson
She confessed that at the height of her career, she was battling depression privately.
She smiled on red carpets but cried in dressing rooms.
She said, "I was tired of being the strong friend."

 Mary J. Blige
Her music became a diary of survival.
She once admitted, "I didn't know what peace felt like."
She was living, performing, succeeding — but barely surviving emotionally.

 Viola Davis
She spent her childhood in trauma and scarcity.
In her memoir she shared, "I didn't feel safe in my own body until adulthood."

 Gabrielle Union
She revealed she had been so conditioned to endure that rest felt like failure.
None of these women lacked strength.
What they lacked was permission to stop performing it.

Signs You've Been Functioning, Not Living

You might be in survival mode if…

- You snap quickly or cry unexpectedly
- You wake up tired even after sleeping
- Peace feels unfamiliar
- You feel guilty resting
- You overdeliver at work because you're scared to disappoint
- You are the friend who pours but rarely receives
- You only feel safe when you're "handling everything"

Survival mode tricks you into believing:

"If I stop, everything will fall apart."

But sis… what if YOU fall apart because you never stop?

What Survival Mode Steals from You!

- Your peace
- Your clarity
- Your joy
- Your softness
- Your femininity
- Your hope
- Your intuition
- Your creativity
- Your ability to receive love
- Your sense of self

Survival mode doesn't just exhaust you.

It erases you — piece by piece.

How You Begin To Escape Survival Mode

This is where the shift begins.

STEP 1: Admit You Are Struggling — Without Shame

Say it aloud:

"I am overwhelmed — and it's okay to not be okay."

You are not weak.

You are not dramatic.

You are not failing.

You are HUMAN.

And even superheroes take their capes off sometimes.

STEP 2: Stop Performing Strength

You do not have to:

- Smile through everything
- Fix everything
- Hold everything
- Pretend everything

Pretending to be unbreakable is the fastest road to breaking.

STEP 3: Rest Before You Are Forced To

Look at Serena Williams.

When she stepped back from tennis — when she said, "I choose me" — the world gasped. She prioritized:

- Her body
- Her peace
- Her motherhood
- Her joy

That wasn't weakness.

That was *strategy*.

Rest is recovery.

Rest is spiritual recalibration.

Rest is strength.

STEP 4: Ask for Help — It's Your New Superpower

Saying "I need help" will save your life.

Your village may include:

- A sister-friend who checks in
- A therapist
- A spiritual mentor
- A supportive coworker
- A family member
- A healing circle

You don't get a badge for doing everything alone.

STEP 5: Slow Down Enough to Hear Yourself

Your intuition cannot compete with your pace.

Your healing cannot catch you if you run.

Your peace cannot locate you if you never sit still.

Stop.

Breathe.

Listen.

You deserve to walk, not sprint, through your life.

STEP 6: Redefine Strength

Real strength says:

- "I deserve rest."
- "I need support."
- "I can't hold everything."
- "I choose peace."

Strength without softness is self-abandonment.

Section Two: The D.A.M.N. Method

Digest. Accept. Move. Note-take.

(A real-life process for surviving hard moments without letting them harden you.)

When life hits you—unexpected loss, betrayal, rejection, public embarrassment, health scares, financial strain: most of us do one of two things:

- **We swallow it** and act "fine"… until we explode later.

- **We obsess over it** and relive it… until it becomes our personality.

The **D.A.M.N. Method** is the middle road:

Feel it fully. Face it honestly. Release it intentionally. Learn from it permanently.

Because a difficult situation doesn't just hurt your feelings, it can hit your **nervous system**, your **self-worth**, your **sleep**, your **appetite**, your **trust**, your **confidence**, your **faith**, your **future choices**.

This method helps you do what healed women do:

- **Digest** what happened (so it doesn't live in your body like poison)
- **Accept** what's true (so you stop negotiating reality)
- **Move** forward (so you don't become stuck in a moment)
- **Note-take** the lesson (so you don't repeat the same pain in a new outfit)

---

1) D — DIGEST

Definition

Digest means: *to process what happened emotionally, mentally, and physically—without rushing, denying, or minimizing it.*

Digesting is **not** dramatizing.

Digesting is **not** staying in it forever.

Digesting is giving your body and spirit permission to say:

"That hurt. That mattered. That changed me."

Why it matters

If you don't digest pain, you don't "get over it."

You **carry it**—in your shoulders, jaw, stomach, sleep, moods, and reactions.

Undigested pain becomes:

- snapping at people who didn't cause the hurt
- overthinking every text, tone, and delay
- being "strong" but secretly numb
- choosing shutdown over vulnerability

- turning into the version of you that is always braced for impact

What Digest looks like (in real, vivid life)

It looks like:

- sitting in your car after work and finally letting the tears come

- staring at a wall because your brain can't make it make sense yet

- eating a little less or sleeping a little more because grief has weight

- replaying the conversation in your head like a movie you didn't audition for

- feeling embarrassed, angry, relieved, devastated—sometimes all in one hour

That is your nervous system saying: **"We took a hit. We need to process."**

How to Digest (tools)

Pick **two** so you don't drown in the moment:

A. Name it (out loud if you can):

- "I feel rejected."
- "I feel betrayed."
- "I feel ashamed."
- "I feel disappointed."

Naming reduces the chaos.

B. Let your body release it:

- cry, walk, stretch, shower, breathe deep, journal, pray

Pain loves stillness when it's uninvited. Move it through.

C. Tell the truth on paper:

Write: "What happened, what it meant to me, and what it triggered."

Example (everyday)

Situation: You didn't get the promotion you worked for.

Digest: You allow yourself to feel the sting—jealousy,

disappointment, anger—without pretending you're "fine." You journal the truth: *"I feel overlooked. I feel tired of proving myself."*

Celebrity example (relatable, not perfect)

• **Simone Biles** stepping back when her mind and body weren't aligned showed a mature form of digesting: listening to what her system needed instead of powering through for applause.

Digest takeaway:

If you don't process it, you will perform it.

---

2) A — ACCEPT

Definition

Accept means: *to stop arguing with reality and face what is true—even when it's painful, unfair, or disappointing.*

Acceptance is not approval.

Acceptance is not weakness.

Acceptance is you saying:

"This is what it is. Now I can decide what I will do."

Why it matters

Many women suffer twice:

1. from what happened
2. from resisting that it happened

Resistance sounds like:

• "I can't believe he would do that." (for the 500th time)
• "If I explain it one more way, they'll finally value me."
• "Maybe if I shrink, it will work again."
• "Maybe I'm asking for too much."

No, sis. You're asking the wrong person.

Acceptance is where power returns—because you stop wasting energy on fantasy.

What Accept looks like (in real, vivid life)

It looks like:

• deleting the paragraph you were about to send because you realize you're begging for clarity
• admitting, *"He's inconsistent."* not *"He's busy."*

- acknowledging, *"This job is changing me."*
- saying, *"They don't respect me here."* and letting it be true
- feeling grief, but choosing not to live in denial

How to Accept (scripts that hold you steady)
- "I don't like it, but I see it."
- "I can't heal what I keep excusing."
- "The pattern is the closure."
- "I accept the truth, and I choose myself."

Example (everyday)

Situation: A friend repeatedly disappears when you need support.

Accept: You stop calling it "they're just going through a lot" and accept: *"This friendship is one-sided."*

Celebrity example

- **Jennifer Lopez** has spoken broadly over the years about learning lessons in love and recognizing when something isn't aligned. That's acceptance: *stopping the story that keeps you stuck.*
- **Meghan Markle** and **Prince Harry** choosing a different life path (regardless of opinions) reflects acceptance of what a situation was costing them.

Accept takeaway:

Acceptance is the moment you stop bleeding from the same wound.

---

3) M — MOVE

Definition

Move means: *to take aligned action forward—even while you're still healing.*
Moving is not "getting over it."
Moving is **getting through it** without letting it become your address.

Why it matters

Some women confuse processing with pausing forever.
But pain that isn't paired with movement turns into:
- stagnation
- bitterness

- fear-based decision-making
- "I'll try again one day…" (and one day never comes)

Movement restores agency. Agency restores confidence.

What Move looks like (in real, vivid life)

It looks like:

- showing up to therapy even when you'd rather scroll and numb out
- applying for new jobs even though rejection embarrassed you last time
- blocking the ex even though your hand shakes while you do it
- going to the gym not to punish your body, but to return to it
- choosing silence instead of explaining yourself to someone committed to misunderstanding you
- taking a deep breath and doing the next right thing—small, steady, consistent

How to Move (3 levels)

Level 1: Micro-moves (today):

- drink water, take a walk, clean one area, send one email, make one call

Level 2: Boundary moves (this week):

- limit access, say no, take space, stop over-functioning

Level 3: Destiny moves (this month):

- enroll, apply, launch, relocate, end it, begin it

Example (everyday)

Situation: You were hurt in a relationship and you're afraid to trust again.

Move: You don't rush into dating. You move by rebuilding your standards, healing your nervous system, and learning to receive safe love.

Celebrity example

- **Megan Thee Stallion** returning to her work and building her life after very public trauma showed movement: continuing to create, grow, and protect herself while still healing.
- **Viola Davis** has described seasons of pushing past fear and limitation to claim space she deserved—movement that matched her worth.

Move takeaway:

You don't need to feel ready to move—moving helps you become ready.

---

4) N — NOTE-TAKE

Definition

Note-take means: *to capture the lesson, the pattern, and the promise—so you don't repeat the pain.*

This is where wisdom is born.

Because if you don't take notes, life will hand you the same test in a different body, a different job, a different zip code.

Why it matters

Note-taking turns pain into:

- discernment
- standards
- boundaries
- better choices
- emotional intelligence

Without notes, you just "move on" and accidentally walk back into the same cycle.

What Note-take looks like (in real, vivid life)

It looks like:

- realizing you ignored your intuition early and promising not to abandon yourself again
- seeing exactly where you started overgiving
- identifying the moment you minimized a red flag because you wanted it to work

- noticing how your body reacted—tight chest, sinking stomach, headaches—before your mind admitted the truth
- writing down what you will *never again* normalize

How to Note-take (the 5 notes every woman needs)

Write these after a difficult situation:

1. **The Trigger:** What happened?
2. **The Pattern:** What has this taught me about them / this environment?
3. **My Part (without shame):** Where did I abandon myself?
4. **The Boundary:** What will I do differently next time?
5. **The Upgrade:** What standard is rising because of this?

Example (everyday)

Situation: You kept dating someone who was inconsistent.

Notes:

- Pattern: inconsistency + excuses
- My part: I accepted crumbs because I wanted potential
- Boundary: I don't build men; I date effort
- Upgrade: consistency is the minimum now

Celebrity example

- **Oprah Winfrey** often speaks about turning experiences into lessons and using them as data for better choices—note-taking energy: extracting wisdom, not just emotion.
- **Beyoncé** has publicly shown reinvention after setbacks and scrutiny—note-taking as strategy: transform the experience into a stronger era.

Note-take takeaway:

A healed woman doesn't just survive it—she learns it.

The D.A.M.N. Method in One Sentence

Digest the pain, Accept the truth, Move with intention, and Note-take the lesson—so your growth becomes permanent.

Use this the next time life hits you:

D — Digest: What am I feeling in my body right now?
A — Accept: What is the truth I keep trying to negotiate?
M — Move: What is the next right step I can take in 24 hours?
N — Note-take: What lesson/standard/boundary is being born here?

Section Three: Stepping Out of the Comfort Zone: When Faith Requires Movement

There are moments in a woman's life when comfort becomes a cage.

After my divorce, I moved back in with my momma for almost two years.

And let me be clear—**that was not failure. That was survival and grace wrapped in one.**

My mother was my **blessing**.

She wasn't in the best of health.

Bad knees and all.

But when it was time for me to prepare my house for the final walkthrough before closing, she stayed with me for **five straight days**.

Five days.

She helped me:

- wash walls
- paint rooms
- pack boxes
- clean every corner

It was just the two of us in that house—two women, tired but determined.

I will never forget that.

At the same time, my mom was watching my son, Jordan, while I:

- worked full-time
- went to night school
- pushed to finish my Master's degree

She was my **lifeline**.

I dragged that woman across **three states**, looking at houses.

And she never complained.

Not once.

Then one day, I found *the house*.

The one.

I knew it the moment I walked in:

This is mine.

Now here's the truth part.

It was slightly out of my price range.

It was an hour away from my job.

I wasn't making a lot of money yet.

But something had shifted in me.

I could feel myself **elevating at work**.

I could feel growth happening internally before it showed up externally.

And instead of talking myself out of it, I did something radical.

I **took a gamble on myself**.

I believed in myself.

I trusted my work ethic.

I trusted my discipline.

I trusted my resilience.

I **bet on me**.

And I got the house.

To this day—not one single day—have I ever been late on that mortgage.

Not once.

That wasn't luck.

That wasn't coincidence.

That was **faith in motion**.

What This Season Taught Me

Comfort feels safe, but comfort rarely grows you.

That season taught me:
- Sometimes security is familiar—but faith is forward.
- Sometimes the next version of your life requires you to move before you feel ready.
- Sometimes you don't need more proof—you need more courage.
- Sometimes believing in yourself looks like doing the scary thing anyway.

Growth will always ask you to:
- leave what's familiar
- trust what you can't fully see yet
- and walk toward yourself with trembling hands and steady faith

And when you do?
Life meets you halfway.

The Lesson for the Reader

Sis, if you're reading this and you're standing at the edge of a decision—
a move,
a career shift,
a boundary,
a dream that scares you—
hear this clearly:
Sometimes faith doesn't look like certainty.
Sometimes it looks like choosing yourself before the evidence arrives.
Comfort didn't build the woman you are becoming.
Courage did.
And the truth is, courage is rarely loud.
It's quiet.
It's shaky.
It's the moment you move anyway—before you feel ready.

This was the season I learned that survival kept me alive…
but movement is what would change my life.
And I was only just beginning to understand what slowing down—
and choosing myself—would actually require.

"God didn't bring me this far to keep me in emergency mode—He brought me here to teach me how to move with intention." – Chanel Brooks

REFLECTION QUESTIONS FOR THE READER

1. Where am I pretending to be okay?
2. Who taught me that rest had to be earned?
3. What am I afraid will happen if I slow down?
4. What would support look like for me right now?
5. What parts of my life feel heavy?
6. What would it look like to choose myself today?

JOURNAL PROMPT: "THE DAY I STOPPED SURVIVING

Write freely about:

- What survival mode has cost you
- What you want to reclaim
- What peace will look like in your next chapter

A FINAL WORD FOR THE WOMAN WHO IS TIRED

Sis…
You have survived storms you had no preparation for.
You've held weight others couldn't carry for five minutes.
You've kept going on nights when your soul wanted to quit.
But your next season is not about survival.
It's about receiving.
Resting.
Breathing.
Becoming.

Expanding.

Reclaiming the softness the world tried to beat out of you.

Because here's the truth:

You are not falling apart — you are finally falling into yourself.

And this time?

You're going to LIVE, not just survive.

Chapter Three

Stop Fighting Battles That Aren't Yours

Yours

(The road to self-discovery)

What I can control and what I can't

INTRODUCTION: THE MOMENT YOU STOP FIGHTING BATTLES THAT AREN'T YOURS IS THE FIRST STEP TO SELF-DISCOVERY

One of the most exhausting things a woman can do is try to control something that will never be hers to hold.

We don't do it on purpose.

We do it because:

- we care deeply
- we want peace
- we want everyone to be okay

- we want outcomes that make sense
- we want to protect ourselves from disappointment
- we want to avoid repeating generational patterns

And somewhere in that mix, we start believing we can control EVERYTHING.

But here's the truth:

"Peace begins the moment you focus only on what belongs to you."

This chapter is about returning to your lane — the lane where your power actually lives — and releasing everything that has been draining you.

Section One: Why Women Struggle With Control (And Don't Even Realize It)

Let's be real:

Women — especially Black women — have been conditioned to:

- manage chaos
- soothe tension
- anticipate needs
- read the room
- hold everyone accountable
- take responsibility for other people's emotional weather

From childhood, we're rewarded for being:

- helpful
- selfless
- accommodating
- forgiving
- flexible
- "the bigger person"

And over time, that conditioning becomes a reflex.

So we try to:

- manage other people's moods
- manage outcomes

- manage relationships
- manage behaviors
- manage their mess

…while ignoring OURS.

Control becomes a coping mechanism when life has given you too many experiences where you felt powerless.

But control is also:

- a thief of peace
- a full-time job without benefits
- a constant source of anxiety

And the worst part?

You cannot control other people —

you can only manage YOUR participation.

Section Two: What You *Cannot* Control — My Real-Life Lessons

You Can't Control How Others Show Up

In boardrooms, county council meetings, public service commission meetings, and community halls, I've spent nearly three decades navigating leadership, advocacy, legislation and community engagement. I've sat in rooms where policy, equity and people's lives intersect. I've crafted strategies, led initiatives, mediated conflict, advised executives and built partnerships that change outcomes for entire communities.

With all that experience, one truth stands out:

I still cannot control everything.

I've been labelled intimidating for having confidence. I've waited (and waited) for the right opportunities or signatures. I've wanted to manage every detail of my son's path. And I've poured love into relationships, projects and communities without always receiving the same energy back.

Every one of those experiences taught me that peace begins when you focus only on what belongs to you. That used to frustrate me. But with growth came understanding:

You can control your diligence.

You cannot control someone else's discipline.

Why Women Struggle with Control (and Don't Even Realize It)

We're conditioned to manage chaos and read rooms. We're rewarded for being helpful, accommodating, flexible and "the bigger person." This constant overfunctioning keeps us exhausted. Perfectionism isn't excellence; it's anxiety that urges us to do more and blame ourselves when others don't carry their weight. Research notes that many women feel they must maintain impossible standards and that asking for help is weakness.

As Hailey Magee explains, people-pleasers often expend too much energy trying to control how others perceive them and too little energy taking responsibility for themselves (haileymagee.com). The result? You attempt to manage other people's emotions, reactions and choices—even when you have zero control over them. And you neglect your own needs, boundaries and wellbeing.

No wonder we're tired.

Real-Life Lessons and Celebrity Parallels

- You can't control how others show up. I've prepared extensively only to watch others appear unprepared. You can control your diligence; you can't control someone else's discipline.
- You can't control how people interpret your confidence. My presence is strong and my voice steady, yet I've been called "too much." Similarly, Michelle Obama has said she realized she couldn't "make" her husband slow down or change; she could only adjust her own expectations and boundaries.
- You can't control the timing of blessings. Waiting for house papers to be signed, for my son's opportunities, or for career

breakthroughs taught me that timing is not my assignment—
alignment is.
- You can't control your son's path. I can advocate for him
and support his dreams, but his becoming belongs to him.
- You can't control reciprocity. My heart is generous—
through mentoring, giving and community service—but I cannot
control whether others give back. I can only choose to love without
losing myself.
Celebrity Lesson: Taraji P. Henson has shared that she stayed in
unhealthy relationships because she saw potential, not patterns, and
eventually realized she couldn't change a partner who didn't want
to change. Mary J. Blige transformed her pain into purpose by
accepting she couldn't rewrite her past but could evolve because of
it. These women illustrate that true power comes from controlling
your own healing and standards—not from fixing others.

.Section Three: Letting Go of Control to Gain Peace

Attempting to control others leads to resistance, resentment and
chronic stress (Thecareercatalyst.co.uk).
Researchers note that 70 % of people live in chronic stress from
trying to control others(Thecareercatalyst.co.uk). Yet the human
brain simply can't control another person's thoughts or actions
(Thecareercatalyst.co.uk).
Instead, shift to emotional responsibility—the art of staying in your
lane with elegance. Focus on your responses, boundaries and
actions. When you do, you'll find that:
- People's behavior no longer dictates your peace.
- You stop chasing closure and start creating it.
- You protect your energy like the sacred resource it is.

I Can't Control How People Interpret My Confidence

My presence is strong.

My voice is steady.

My leadership is magnetic.

And yes—my confidence fills a room.

But not everyone knows what to do with a woman who is sure of who she is.

I've been labeled intimidating, "intense," or "too much"—when in reality, I was simply walking in my purpose.

You can't control their insecurities or misunderstandings.

But you *can* control staying true to your calling.

I Can't Control the Timing of Blessings

Whether it was:

- waiting for the house papers to be signed,
- waiting for the right career opening,
- waiting for a project to finally get approved,
- waiting for a personal prayer to be answered,
- or waiting for your own strength to return…

I've learned that timing is not your assignment.

Alignment is.

Breakthroughs don't arrive early, and they don't arrive late.

They arrive when you're ready for the version of you that comes after the breakthrough.

I Can't Control My Son's Entire Path

As a mother, there's nothing I want more than to see my son grow into the fullness of who he is. I've advocated for him, celebrated his wins, guided his decisions, and supported his dreams—especially his passion for football.

But I can't control:

- which opportunities arise for him,
- who notices his talent,
- or how his journey unfolds.

I can influence.
I can pray.
I can support.
But the becoming?
That's his.

I Can't Control Reciprocity

My heart is generous—whether it's community service, mentoring, giving, lifting other women up, or pouring into my networks.
And still…
not everyone gives back with the same energy.
I can't control their capacity.
But I *can* control how I continue to love without losing myself.

Section Four: What I *Can* Control — My Superpowers in Action

Now let's talk about the areas where I've *have* reclaimed my power. These are the elements that make me not just resilient—but unstoppable.

I Control My Voice

I have the ability to walk into any room—boardroom, community meeting, legislative session, or sister circle—and articulate vision with clarity and authority.
I can't control who listens.
But I *do* control how y speak truth, advocate, and lead.
And I do it exceptionally.

I Control My Boundaries

I've learned to protect my time, my peace, my weekends, and my emotional space.
I've stopped overextending.
Stopped overcommitting.
Stopped pleasing at the expense of my own well-being.
I decide who gets access to the best parts of you.

I Control How I Heal and Rest

I intentionally chose the retreat.
I intentionally unplugged.
I intentionally allowed myself to breathe.
And when life sent that "missing orange suitcase" moment, it was the universe's nudge:
"Slow down, Sis. Really slow down."
Rest is not weakness for me—it is strategic preparation.

I Control My Career Ambition

When opportunities arise, I don't wait for permission.
I apply.
I elevate.
I stretch.
I grow.
I envision bigger.
Whether it's an executive role, a transformational program, a leadership opportunity, or a groundbreaking team contributing to the future of AI—I position myself with purpose.
I can't control when the offer comes.
But I *absolutely* control how I prepare for it.

I Control My Financial Vision

From my crypto investments

to my pre-IPO shares

to the crypto I created movement—

I am building generational wealth with intentionality.

I can't control market volatility.

But I *can* control my strategy, my learning, and my belief in my own

capacity.

I Control My Inner Voice

This is one of my greatest strengths.

My self-talk has transformed from survival-mode whispers into a

warrior-woman anthem.

I've traded:

- "I'm overwhelmed"

for

- "I'm evolving."

I've traded:

- "I'm tired of fighting"

for

- "I'm built for this."

I've traded:

- "Why me?"

for

- "Watch me."

And THAT is where the power lives.

Why This Matters

By recognizing what you can and cannot control, you are no longer:

- drained by other people's choices,
- weighed down by timelines,
- overwhelmed by uncertainty,

- • or stuck in cycles of over-responsibility.

Instead, you become the highest, most aligned version of yourself.

A woman who:

✦ Protects her peace

✦ Moves with clarity

✦ Speaks with authority

✦ Heals with intention

✦ Leads with purpose

✦ Receives with grace

This is what Chapter Three teaches:

Real power is not controlling the world—
real power is controlling your world.

And you, Sis, are doing exactly that.

"When a woman stops trying to control the world around her and starts mastering the world within her, she becomes a force no chaos can shake." – Chanel Brooks

Because, Sis…

It is not your job to fix what you did not break.

Section Five: The Power Zone Framework (Your New Life Tool)

You only control **three things** in this life:

1. Your Actions

What you choose to do.

What you choose NOT to do.

2. Your Attitude

Your reaction, your energy, your perspective.

3. Your Boundaries

What you allow, permit, accept, or reject.

That's it.

Everything else?

Outside your zone.

This chapter teaches you how to stay in your lane — your **power zone** — where you operate from strength, clarity, and peace.

The Areas You *Think* You Can Control, (But Can't)

Let's break these down with *real-life examples* and *celebrity parallels* to show you how universal this struggle is.

✗ 1. Other People's Behavior

You can't control how your partner, friend, coworker, or family member behaves.

Example (Your Life):

At work, you can show up with professionalism, clarity, and integrity —

but you cannot control:

- other people's egos
- their agendas
- their leadership style
- their personality clashes

Still, for years you carried THEIR dysfunction like it was YOUR responsibility.

That ends here.

Celebrity Parallel:

Michelle Obama famously said she learned that she couldn't "make" Barack slow down, rest, or change — she could only adjust *her own* expectations and boundaries.

✗ 2. Other People's Healing

You cannot drag someone into their breakthrough.

You cannot:

- force a man to grow up

- make someone communicate
- make someone choose you
- make a friend be loyal
- make a coworker behave ethically
- make a family member go to therapy

Celebrity Parallel:

Taraji P. Henson said she stayed in relationships longer than she should because she saw their *potential*, not their *patterns*.

Sound familiar?

✖ 3. The Past

Sis, you can replay it, reanalyze it, reread it…

but you cannot rewrite it.

What you *can* do is:

- learn from it
- grow from it
- refuse to repeat it

Celebrity Example:

Mary J. Blige turned her pain into purpose by finally accepting that she couldn't change her past — but she could evolve because of it.

✖ 4. Other People's Opinions

People will talk regardless.

You cannot control:

- how they perceive you
- what they assume
- what they choose to believe
- what version of you they hold onto

But you CAN control how much access you give them.

✖ 5. The Timing of Your Breakthrough

You can prepare, but you cannot control the *when*.

Example (Your Life):

When you were applying for certain roles…
When you were waiting for your next season…
When you prayed for your husband…
God made you wait — because the version of YOU needed for the blessing wasn't ready yet.
And when you DID become that version?
You met Donoven.
Timing isn't random.
It's strategic.

The Areas You *Can* Control (The Power Zone)
Now let's shift into the GOOD part — where your power actually lives.

✓ 1. Your Standards
You decide:

- what treatment is acceptable
- what behavior is intolerable
- what energy is welcome
- what dynamics end today

Your life changes when your standards rise.

✓ 2. Your Boundaries
A boundary is not a wall.
It's a door — *you choose who gets access.*
Real-life example (Me):
I learned to stop overextending myself professionally and personally.
The moment I did?
My peace increased.
My confidence increased.
My joy returned.
My relationships aligned.

✔ 3. My Reactions

People can TRY you…
but they cannot MAKE you.
You control:

- your tone
- your energy
- your emotional investment
- your decision to engage or disengage

✔ 4. Your Self-Talk

Sis, the voice in your head runs your life.
If you talk to yourself like an enemy…
you will live like one.
You control whether to speak with:

- grace
- compassion
- patience
- encouragement

✔ 5. Your Habits + Choices

Transformation is not magic.
It's repetition.
You control:

- what you consume (food, social media, conversations)
- who you spend time with
- how you speak over yourself
- your consistency
- your discipline

Section Six: The Shift: Letting Go of Control to Gain Peace

You don't achieve peace by controlling everything.

You achieve peace by **controlling your response to everything.**

This is called **Emotional Responsibility** —

the art of staying in your lane with elegance and power.

When you master it:

- People's behavior no longer disrupts your day
- You don't chase closure — you create it
- You don't internalize attitudes — you filter them
- You stop trying to fix grown adults
- You walk away from what drains you
- You protect your energy like a sacred resource

This is womanhood at its highest form.

REFLECTION QUESTIONS FOR THE READER

1. **What am I trying to control that is not mine to carry?**
2. **What drains me because I won't release it?**
3. **Where am I abandoning myself while trying to save others?**
4. **What would happen if I chose peace instead of control?**
5. **Who or what do I need to give back to God?**

EXERCISE: "THE POWER ZONE MAP"

Draw two circles.

Circle 1: Things I Cannot Control

Fill it with:

- people
- outcomes
- timing
- behavior
- opinions

Circle 2: My Power Zone
Fill it with:
- boundaries
- actions
- choices
- reactions
- my healing
- my energy
- my effort

This visual changes EVERYTHING.

So Why Is This Important for Your Next Level?

Because your **I AM HER** identity requires a new level of emotional maturity.

You cannot:
- control a man into loving right
- control a job into valuing you
- control a family member into healing
- control the timing of your elevation

But you CAN control:
- your expectations
- your standards
- your vision
- your discipline
- your access list
- and your response

This is sovereignty.
This is womanhood.
This is HER energy.

CLOSING QUOTE OF THE CHAPTER

"A powerful woman doesn't control the world —
she controls her space within it." Chanel Brooks

✦ Chapter Four
"No Is a Complete Sentence"
(Put YOU First, Sis — Without Apology.)

INTRODUCTION: THE UNCOMFORTABLE GIFT OF GROWTH

This chapter is about to step on some toes, free some souls, snatch some wigs, and restore some boundaries ALL at the same time

There comes a moment in every woman's life — a quiet, sacred, soul-deep moment — when she realizes:

"This no longer fits."

Not in a dramatic, movie-scene kind of way.

Not in a meltdown.

Not in a storm.

But in a whisper.

A nudge.

A tightening in the spirit.

It might be:

- a job you once prayed for
- a relationship you once fought for
- a friendship you once clung to
- a habit that once comforted you
- a role you once mastered
- a version of you that once protected you

Letting go doesn't always come with tears or arguments.

Sometimes the release is as gentle as an exhale:

"I can't stay where I no longer belong."

This chapter is about honoring the truth your spirit already knows.

It's about recognizing what's expired, blessing what helped you grow, and stepping into what's waiting for you next.

Because release is not loss —

it's elevation.

Section One: Signs You've Outgrown Something (or Someone)

Women often stay too long because we confuse *familiarity* with *belonging*.

But the soul?

The soul never lies.

Here are the unmistakable signals your spirit has moved ahead of your life:

1. Peace Leaves First

Peace is intuitive.

Peace will retreat before you consciously admit the truth.

Examples:

- You dread logging into your job, even though you used to thrive there.
- Conversations with certain friends now feel draining instead of nourishing.

- A relationship that once felt warm now feels like walking barefoot on gravel.
- Your spirit feels tight, restricted, and restless.

Your peace is your compass.

When it leaves?

Your spirit already has.

Celebrity Example:

Meghan Markle shared that she felt peace leave long before she and Harry stepped away from royal duties. Her truth arrived before her circumstances caught up.

---

2. You Start Feeling Irritated by What You Used to Tolerate

It's not moodiness.

It's awakening.

Your soul is rejecting what no longer aligns.

Old patterns feel suffocating.

Old excuses no longer soothe you.

Old cycles feel insulting to your new self-awareness.

This discomfort is divine.

The Universe irritates you out of your comfort zone so you won't settle there.

Celebrity Example:

Issa Rae admitted she couldn't tolerate certain Hollywood "norms" anymore. Her irritation became the push that led her into her mogul era.

---

3. You Don't Recognize Yourself in That Space Anymore

You've expanded.

Your environment hasn't.

Your:

- values
- standards
- purpose
- identity

…have all outgrown the container they were once in.

Outgrown spaces feel like trying to wear clothes two sizes too small.

Celebrity Example:

Michelle Obama said there were seasons as First Lady where she didn't recognize herself — and that realization helped her reclaim her identity in her own terms.

---

4. Conversations No Longer Feed You

When you're evolving, drama tastes bitter.

When you're elevating, gossip sounds childish.

When you're healing, chaos feels foreign.

You start craving depth, purpose, vision, clarity.

When silence feels more nourishing than the conversations around you?

You've outgrown the circle.

Celebrity Example:

Oprah famously shifted her social circle when her growth demanded deeper alignment, not louder noise.

---

5. You Keep Asking for Signs You Already Have

Sis…

When you pray for clarity but ignore the flags already waving?

That's not confusion.

That's attachment.

Release is overdue.

Celebrity Example:

Jennifer Lopez said the signs were always there in relationships that didn't serve her — she just wasn't ready to let go yet. Her evolution began when she finally listened.

Section Two: Why Letting Go Feels So Hard

You're not grieving the person or the position…

You're grieving:
- the identity you wore
- the version of you that survived there
- the comfort of familiarity
- the predictability of routine
- the illusion of safety
- the fear of who you'll be without it

Letting go forces you to confront:
- loneliness
- disappointment
- change
- uncertain futures
- your own growth

Release requires courage.

But staying requires self-abandonment.

Growth always demands a funeral.

A burial of what you've outgrown so you can resurrect into who you're becoming.

Section Three: Real-Life Examples (Inspired by Me)

These are NOT hypotheticals — this is my real evolution.

✦ 1. I've Outgrew Being the "Fixer Friend"

You were everybody's emergency hotline.

Everybody's life raft.

Everybody's therapist.

Once my spirit evolved, that role felt like emotional captivity.

My boundaries rose.

My energy elevated.

That wasn't selfish —

that was graduation.

2. I've Outgrew Spaces That Couldn't Hold My Leadership

My brilliance became too big for certain rooms.
My wisdom too seasoned.
My voice too strong.
I stopped shrinking so others could feel comfortable.
That wasn't arrogance —
that was alignment.

3. I've Outgrew Relationships Where I Had to Over-Function

If one person is doing the emotional labor for two?
It's not partnership.
It's parenting.
I've released the version of me that worked harder than the connection deserved.

4. I've Outgrew Patterns I Once Normalized

Running on empty.
Fixing everything.
Overcommitting.
Ignoring intuition.
That was the old identity.
I stepped into my soft era —
the healed version of you who chooses alignment, not exhaustion.

5. I've Outgrew the Version of Me Who Dimmed Her Shine

Now?
I walk in:
- intention
- elegance

- luxury
- softness
- self-trust
- loud peace
- quiet power

I no longer fit inside the woman I used to be.

Section Four: The Release Ritual — How to Let Go Gracefully

Letting go doesn't have to be explosive or messy.
It can be sacred.
Here's your blueprint:

✦ STEP 1: Tell the Truth (No Sugarcoating)

Write down:
"What exactly no longer aligns with who I'm becoming?"
Say it plainly.
Name it clearly.
Truth is liberation.

✦ STEP 2: Honor What It Once Gave You

Before you close the door, acknowledge the gift.
It taught you something.
It grew you.
It shaped you.
Release with gratitude, not resentment.

✦ STEP 3: Detach From the Potential & Accept the Pattern

Say it with me:
Potential is a fantasy.
Patterns are facts.

You don't release potential —
you release what someone consistently *shows you.*

STEP 4: Set the Boundary That Matches Your Evolution

A real boundary might look like:

- limiting access
- ending communication
- stepping back
- stepping forward into something new
- reducing emotional labor

Boundaries are not punishment.
They're self-respect.

STEP 5: Fill the Space With Something Healthy

Releasing creates a vacuum.
You MUST fill it intentionally.
Replace:

- stress → rest
- chaos → clarity
- overgiving → reciprocity
- fear → faith
- old habits → elevated standards

Empty hands receive nothing.
Open hands receive everything.

STEP 6: Speak the Release Declaration

Say this out loud:
"I release what no longer serves me, so I can rise into what was always meant for me."
Say it until it settles into your spirit.

Section Five: What Happens After You Release (The Glow-Up Phase)

You want the secrets behind every woman's glow-up?

Here it is:

Release.

Because the MOMENT you release…

- Peace returns
- Clarity unlocks
- Energy rises
- Opportunities appear
- Self-respect multiplies
- Your circle upgrades
- Your intuition sharpens
- Your spirit breathes again
- Your glow becomes undeniable

Releasing doesn't empty your life.

It aligned your life.

The Universe rearranges itself in your favor the moment your hands are free.

Letting go is not losing —

Letting go is making room.

Section Six: Homework — The Let-It-Go Liberation Plan

Homework #1: Write 5 Things You Know You've Outgrown

Don't censor this.

Homework #2: Identify the Emotional Attachment

Next to each one, write:

"What am I REALLY afraid of letting go?"

Homework #3: Write a Release Letter

To a person, a habit, or a former version of you.

You don't have to send it.

But you DO have to release it.

Homework #4: Replace It With ONE New Behavior

A new boundary, habit, standard, affirmation, or environment.

Homework #5: Daily Release Mantra

Say this for 7 days:

"I do not chase.

I do not cling.

I release with love,

and I rise with purpose."

The Church of No

Welcome to a sacred space, Sis.

Go ahead and repeat after me:

"No… is a complete sentence."

See?

No lightning struck.

No relationship ended instantly.

No universe collapsed.

You are still here.

You are still loved.

You are still HER.

Somewhere between little girl and grown woman, many of us were taught that "No" is:

- rude
- selfish
- ungrateful
- unladylike

So we learned to:

- over-explain
- over-apologize
- over-function

We swallowed our truth and dressed it up as "it's fine."

But here's the reality:

Saying yes to everything is the quickest way to lose yourself. Saying no is the quickest way to find yourself again.

This chapter is about rebuilding your boundaries, reclaiming your time and energy, and resigning from your role as the unpaid emotional staff for every job, friend group, family crisis, and especially for men you keep enrolling in your **Science Fair of Potential.**

Let's Call It What It Is — Women Overgive. Period.

From childhood, we were praised for being:

- "helpful"
- "nice"
- "cooperative"
- "selfless"
- "the good girl"

We were trained to measure our value by how much we did for others.

Nobody told us this:

Selfless women eventually become resentful women.

Section One: Professionally: Overbooked, Undervalued, and Over It

Picture this:

Your calendar looks like a game of Tetris.

Back-to-back meetings.

You're the go-to person when something goes wrong.

Your boss:

"Can you take this on? You're just so good at handling things."

You say yes to:

- the extra assignment

- the committee work
- planning the office celebration
- fixing your coworker's sloppy work
- mentoring the new hire
- being the "calm, strong" one in every crisis

You do it because:

- You don't want to seem unhelpful.
- You're afraid saying no will impact your review.
- You've been told "you're so good with people."

But here's the gag:

- You're exhausted.
- You aren't being compensated.
- You aren't being promoted.
- And half of what you're doing doesn't move your career forward at ALL.

If you died today, beloved, a job posting would be up before the flowers on your casket wilted.

Professional Reframe:

High performers set boundaries.

Leaders prioritize.

People who last say "no" strategically.

Your worth at work is not measured by how much you tolerate—it's measured by how clearly you operate.

Section Two: Personally: Friends, Family & Everybody's Emergency Hotline

Some of y'all need to change your voicemail to:

"If this is a crisis YOU created, please hang up and figure it out like an adult." 😌

You say yes to:

- watching someone's kids last-minute
- loaning money you actually need

- being the unofficial family therapist
- hosting every holiday
- planning every birthday
- being the "strong one" everyone vents to

But who checks on you?

Who says:

- "Do YOU need anything?"
- "How can I support YOU?"
- "You can rest. I'll handle this."

Exactly.

Real talk:

It is not selfish to refuse what drains you.

It is self-preservation.

Section Three: Relationships: Sis, Stop Turning Men into Science Projects

Buckle up, because now we're in the lab.

Women have a dangerous habit:

We turn men into **projects**.

We see:

- potential
- charm
- brokenness
- "he just needs a good woman" syndrome

And suddenly we're:

- his mother
- his therapist
- his career coach
- his health coach
- his legal advisor
- his prayer warrior
- his HR department
- his probation officer

You went on one date and somehow you're already:

"Helping him heal his childhood trauma, rewrite his resume, fix his credit, strengthen his relationship with God, and rebuild his self-esteem."

Girl. Put. The. Clipboard. DOWN.

This is not:

- Biology 101
- Build-A-Man Workshop
- Emotional Rehab Center

And you are not **Dr. Fix-It-All.**

Key Truth:

If a man does not WANT to change, you cannot MAKE him change.

- Your determination can't override his disinterest.
- Your loyalty can't override his lack of effort.
- Your prayers can't override his procrastination.
- Your love can't override his laziness.
- Your analysis of his *potential* cannot override his *patterns*.

Real-Life Scenario:

You're dating a man who:

- says he "isn't ready for a relationship"
- forgets plans
- communicates only when it benefits him
- calls when he's bored or lonely

But you tell yourself:

- "He's been hurt before."
- "He just needs someone to show him real love."
- "He's dealing with a lot right now."

So you keep pouring, explaining, waiting… hoping the next version of him will finally choose you correctly.

Meanwhile, he's not confused.

He's comfortable.

SIS: You are not confused either—you're just ignoring what's clear.

Celebrity Parallel: Ciara and the Prayer
Before Russell Wilson, Ciara had relationships that played out in front of the world. She had to learn to stop being a rehab center for emotionally unavailable men and start being a sanctuary for herself. Once she raised her standards and asked for a love that matched her, not drained her, her prayer was answered.
That's not magic.
That's **boundaries.**

Why We Do This — The Emotional Truth

We become emotional scientists because:

- We see the GOOD in people.
- We're naturally nurturing.
- We believe love is proven by how much we endure.
- We feel responsible for other people's growth.
- We're afraid of being "mean" or "giving up."
- We think being chosen means being needed.

But here's the reality:

Helping people who refuse to help themselves is not love — it's self-abandonment.

You are not disloyal for letting go of a man who won't grow.

You are not cold for setting boundaries with family.

You are not selfish for declining unpaid emotional labor.

You are finally saying:

"I matter here too."

Professional Advice — Saying No Without Burning Bridges

Let's be practical. Saying "no" at work doesn't mean being combative. It means being clear.

Use the "Priorities" Conversation

Instead of just "No," try:

"I'm at capacity with X, Y and Z. Which of these would you like me to deprioritize to make room for this new task?"

This does two things:

- Puts responsibility back on leadership to decide what's most important.
- Signals that you're not an endless well of free labor.

Use Email Scripts

Script 1 – Extra Project

"Thank you for thinking of me for this. Given my current workload on A and B, I wouldn't be able to give this the level of attention it deserves. I'll need to pass this time."

Script 2 – Emotional Support Role

"I value being a supportive teammate, but I'm not the best person to handle this. You might want to connect with HR / EAP / [another resource]."

Protect Your Off Hours

Your off time is not "flex time" for other people's emergencies. You are allowed to:

- log off
- mute work chats
- ignore non-urgent texts
- say, "Let's talk about this Monday."

Simone Biles choosing her mental and emotional health over the Olympics was a global reminder that even at the highest level, protecting yourself is not weakness—it's wisdom.

How to Break the Cycle — Step-by-Step

Start with "Micro-No's"

Small no's build big confidence.

- "No, I can't talk right now—can we schedule another time?"
- "No, I'm not available this weekend."
- "No, that doesn't work for me."

Say it without overexplaining.

You are not a customer service representative for your own life.

Stop Explaining the "No"

You do not owe:

- a sad story
- a health update
- a financial breakdown
- a "maybe next time"

You are allowed to simply say:

"That doesn't work for me."

"I'm unable to do that."

"No, thank you."

The moment you stop explaining, you stop negotiating your worth.

Ask: "What Does This Cost ME?"

Before you say yes, ask:

- Will this drain me?
- Will this inconvenience my schedule or rest?
- Will I resent this later?
- Am I doing this out of guilt, fear, or obligation?

If the cost is your peace…

It's too expensive.

Let Men Be Grown Adults

Repeat after me:

"It is NOT my job to raise a man somebody else already raised."

If he:

- is inconsistent
- disappears when life gets hard
- doesn't do the bare minimum
- has no plan for his own life

That's not a challenge.

That's your cue.

A man who wants to be better will upgrade HIMSELF. You are a partner, not a probation officer.

Release Responsibility for Other People's Growth

You are not:

- the fixer
- the savior
- the glue
- the human band-aid
- the family's emotional sponge

You are allowed to love people and still refuse to carry what they refuse to heal.

You can support someone's journey without sacrificing yourself on their altar.

Build a "Yes to Me" List

Make a list of what you're saying **yes** to going forward:

- Yes to rest
- Yes to quiet mornings
- Yes to therapy or coaching
- Yes to joyful experiences
- Yes to reciprocal relationships
- Yes to being compensated for your value
- Yes to saying "I'll think about it" instead of automatic yes

Everything else?

Auto-decline with love.

Real-Life Transformation — When "No" Changed Everything

Think about my life:

- The job I finally left

- • The friendship I quietly backed away from
- • The man I stopped trying to fix
- • The family pattern I refused to repeat

Remembering how terrified I was to say no…

and how much lighter I felt after I did.

It was *my* no that created space for:

- • new opportunities
- • healthy love
- • deeper peace
- • my husband, Donoven
- • my elevation

My "no" didn't close doors.

It redirected you to the right ones.

Practice Scripts – "No" in Real Time

To a man who wants access without commitment:

"No, this doesn't work for me anymore."

To a friend who only calls when they need something:

"No, I can't take that on right now."

To a boss piling on extra work:

"No, that won't fit into my workload as it stands. What would you like me to pause to take this on?"

To family who overstep:

"No, that doesn't work for me. I hope you can respect that."

To yourself when you're about to overextend:

"No, we're not doing that today. We're choosing rest."

Sexy, Sacred Soulwork — Your Homework

The Selfish Woman Starter Kit

Write down **10 things** you are saying **NO** to this month.

Examples:

- • No to being the default fixer.
- • No to last-minute chaos.

- No to emotionally unavailable men.
- No to unpaid emotional labor.
- No to drained, one-sided friendships.
- No to showing up exhausted and calling it "loyalty."
- No to saying yes just so people will like you.

Ten Things You're Saying YES To

Examples:

- Yes to rest and naps.
- Yes to unplugging from your phone.
- Yes to long baths, skincare, and softness.
- Yes to pursuing your goals.
- Yes to decline invitations that don't excite you.
- Yes to high-value relationships.
- Yes to being cherished, not tolerated.

Identify ONE Relationship Where You've Been the Scientist

Ask yourself:

- What am I trying to fix?
- What am I hoping he becomes?
- What am I ignoring about who he actually is?
- What would I do if I stopped trying to change him?

Write it.

Face it.

Release it.

Mirror Work: Saying No Out Loud

Stand in the mirror and say:

- "No. I'm not available."
- "No. That doesn't align with my peace."
- "No. I don't have the emotional capacity for that."
- "No. I choose me this time."

Notice how your body feels when you say it.

That's not guilt.

That's power waking up.

REFLECTION QUESTIONS FOR THE READER

1. Where have I been saying yes out of fear instead of desire?
2. Who benefits from my lack of boundaries?
3. Who would actually adjust if I started saying no?
4. Which man did I turn into a science project, and what did it cost me?
5. Where in my life do I repeatedly abandon myself?
6. What is one "no" I can give this week that will set my future self free?

"NO WEEK" CHALLENGE

For the next **7 days:**

- Say **NO** once a day to something that drains you.
- No explanation.
- No apology.

Write down:

- What you said no to
- How it felt
- What changed because you didn't overextend

Watch your peace expand in real time.

FINAL AFFIRMATION

"I honor what was, release what no longer aligns, and welcome the fullness of who I am becoming."
— *Chanel Brooks*

Chapter Five

THE REBIRTH OF YOUR IDENTITY

(Who You Were, Who You Became, and Who You're Becoming)

INTRODUCTION: DO NOT ALLOW OTHERS TO DEFINE YOU

(You Are the Author — Not the Audience)

There comes a moment in every woman's evolution when she must make a decision:

Will I live the story others write about me — or the one I choose for myself?

Too many women unknowingly surrender authorship of their lives to:

- family expectations
- societal timelines
- cultural stereotypes
- workplace labels
- relationship roles
- past mistakes

- other people's comfort

And without realizing it, they begin living a narrative that was never theirs.

Let me say this clearly, loudly, and lovingly:

This is YOUR life.

YOU are the author.

Everyone else is a supporting character — at best.

Section One: Other People's Definitions Are Often Projections

People define you based on:

- who you used to be
- what they needed you to be
- how you made them feel
- what benefited them
- what scared them about your growth

Their version of you is rarely rooted in truth.

It's rooted in **their limitations, jealousy, fear, or convenience.**

And when you outgrow that version?

They struggle — because your evolution disrupts the story they were comfortable telling.

Section Two: You Don't Need Permission to Rewrite Your Life

You are allowed to:

- change your mind
- change your direction
- change your standards
- change your pace
- change your identity

Growth is not betrayal.
Evolution is not arrogance.
Reinvention is not instability.
It is **self-respect**.

Celebrity Proof: Women Who Refused to Be Defined
Oprah Winfrey
Oprah was told:
- she was too emotional
- too Black
- too poor
- too damaged

She refused every label placed on her — and authored a life of influence, wealth, and purpose **on her own terms**.
She didn't become Oprah by fitting in.
She became Oprah by **deciding who she was**.

Viola Davis
Hollywood tried to define Viola as:
- "too dark"
- "too serious"
- "not marketable"

She rewrote the narrative by choosing depth, excellence, and truth.
She once said she stopped waiting for permission and started **claiming space**.
That's authorship.

Michelle Obama
Michelle was boxed as:
- "Barack's wife"
- "too intimidating"
- "too outspoken"

Instead of shrinking, she expanded.
She reclaimed her identity beyond the role and showed the world

that **you can honor your past chapters without being confined to them.**

Mary J. Blige
Mary was defined by:
- pain
- heartbreak
- survival

Until she decided:
"I am not my trauma. I am my healing."
Her *Good Morning Gorgeous* era wasn't a rebrand — it was **a reclamation.**

Section Three: Your Life Is Not a Group Project

Everyone will have opinions.
Everyone will have commentary.
Everyone will think they know what's best for you.
But here's the truth:
No one lives with your consequences but YOU.
Not your friends.
Not your family.
Not your ex.
Not society.
Not the critics.
So why let them write your story?

Signs You've Been Living Someone Else's Narrative

- You explain your choices too much
- You feel guilty for wanting more
- You shrink your dreams to keep peace

- You stay in roles that no longer fit
- You fear judgment more than regret

That's not intuition.

That's conditioning.

Reclaiming Authorship: How You Take Your Power Back

1. Decide Who You Are — On Purpose

Stop asking:

"What do they think?"

Start asking:

"What feels true to me now?"

2. Release Old Labels

Just because someone met you in one chapter doesn't mean they get to narrate the next.

3. Speak Your Life Into Existence

Words matter.

Stories matter.

Identity matters.

Speak with intention:

- "I am evolving."
- "I choose differently now."
- "This chapter is mine."

4. Let People Be Uncomfortable

Your growth will offend people who benefited from your silence.

Let them adjust.

5. Edit Ruthlessly

Every author edits.

So must you.

Edit:

- access
- expectations
- relationships
- obligations

Protect the storyline.

A Truth Every Woman Needs to Hear

You don't owe consistency to people who only know a previous version of you.

You owe honesty to yourself.

Your past does not get veto power over your future.

Affirmation

"I release every version of myself that was written for survival.

I step fully into the story I choose to live.

I am the author of my life — and I write with intention, courage, and grace."

Section Four: The Funeral You Didn't Know You Needed

There comes a moment in every woman's life when she looks at herself—really looks—and whispers:

"I'm not the me I used to be…

but I'm not yet the me I'm meant to become."

That moment is not loud.

It doesn't post itself on Instagram.

It doesn't always come with tears.

It's a quiet identity earthquake.

A spiritual in-between.

On a soul level, it feels like:

- a funeral for your old identity, and
- a soft birth for the new one.

Here's the truth:

Some versions of you have to die so the real you can finally live.
Not:

- the people-pleasing you
- the overworking you
- the shrinking-for-love you
- the "I'll fix him" you
- the "I don't need help" you
- the "I'll settle because I'm tired" you

But the TRUE YOU—whole, grounded, feminine, joyful, powerful—has been waiting her turn.

This chapter is her entrance.

The Old Identity – What You Outgrew Without Realizing It

Identity is not always chosen.
Sometimes it's assigned.

- By family.
- By culture.
- By trauma.
- By survival.
- By other people's expectations.

Women often wear roles that expired years ago—but we keep them on because we don't know who we'd be without them.

Here are some of the identities you may have outgrown:

✦ The Hero
"I'll save everyone. I'll carry everybody's load."
You jump in, you fix, you rescue—even when no one asked you to.
You became the family's 911, the office fixer, the friend who is "always there."
But heroes rarely rest.
And eventually, even heroes collapse.

✦ The Strong One

"I'll never break. I'll never need anything."
You were the one people leaned on—but never leaned *to*.
You didn't cry in front of people.
You didn't ask for help.
You thought strength meant silence.
But that silence was suffocating your soul.

✦ The Love Prover
"If I love harder, they'll treat me better."
You overgive in relationships:
You show up. You give chances. You pour and pour and pour.
You think:
- "If I'm more patient…"
- "If I'm more understanding…"
- "If I prove I'm loyal…"

…then he'll finally show up right.
But real love doesn't require you to beg for bare minimum.

✦ The Fixer
"I can change him. I can heal him. I can help him evolve."
You meet potential and move in like it's your job.
You become his healer, planner, therapist, life coach and spiritual advisor.
We talked about this in the Science Project chapter—but it matters here too:
You are not a rehabilitation center for grown men.

✦ The Overachiever
"If I achieve more, I'll be valued more."
You stacked degrees, certifications, titles.
You led committees, chaired boards, ran initiatives.
On paper: impressive.
In your spirit: exhausted.

Your identity was tied to "doing" instead of "being."

✦ The Peacekeeper
"I don't want to upset anyone."
You avoid conflict like it's fire.
You hold your tongue.
You absorb disrespect and call it "keeping the peace."
But if *your* peace is the sacrifice, that's not peace—that's suppression.

✦ The Silent Sufferer
"I'll just deal with it."
You raised your tolerance on everything:
- pain
- disrespect
- inconvenience
- emotional neglect

You convinced yourself: "It's not that bad."
Meanwhile, your spirit is screaming, "It *is* that bad."
Does any of this sound familiar?
Yeah… it's time for the funeral.

Section Five: Survival You vs. Evolved You

There is:
- the version of you that survived, and
- the version of you that is meant to thrive.

They are NOT the same woman.

💔 Survival You
Survival You:
- overworks to feel worthy
- overgives to feel loved
- overexplains to feel understood
- stays quiet to avoid conflict

- says yes when she means no
- hides pain so she won't feel like a burden
- tolerates too much and calls it loyalty
- stays in rooms she has outgrown because leaving is scary
- tries to control everything so she won't be disappointed again

Survival You wasn't wrong.
She did what she had to do.
Honor her.
Thank her.
But don't stay her.

🌱 Evolved You

Evolved You:

- rests without apology
- says no without overexplaining
- speaks truth even when her voice shakes
- chooses peace over chaos, clarity over confusion
- holds standards and doesn't negotiate them mid-relationship
- walks away from misalignment—even when it's comfortable
- protects her energy like it's currency (because it is)
- chooses HER, not in a selfish way, but in a self-honoring way

You are not "changing" into someone else.
You are *becoming* someone you already were—beneath the layers of survival.

What Triggered Your Rebirth?

Every rebirth has a catalyst.
Something shook you and said: "We can't keep living like this."

Here are examples pulled from *my* journey and the journeys of many women:

1. When Life Knocked the Strength Out of Me

That night in September 2006…

- Bank account almost empty.
- Mortgage behind.
- Daycare due.
- Gas tank on E.

I cried the kind of cry that comes from the bones.

I wasn't just tired.

I was at capacity.

It felt like everything was falling apart.

But spiritually?

That was the exact night Life said:

"Enough. This version of you cannot go with you where I'm taking you."

It was the beginning of my rebirth.

---

2. When I Outgrew Roles I Once Mastered

There was a time when:

- policy rooms energized me
- community work lit me up
- being "the go-to person" felt like purpose

But then:

- the meetings started draining me
- the politics felt heavy
- the obligations started to outweigh the fulfillment

I realized: "I love impact… but not like this anymore."

That's not ingratitude—that's evolution.

---

3. When I Started Choosing Rest Over Reputation

That retreat at the mansion.

- The laughter.

- The stillness.
- The joy.
- The orange suitcase left behind.

On the surface, I forgot luggage.
On a soul level?
The Universe tapped me and said:
"You are still rushing. Slow down. Be present. Become again."
Rest stopped being a luxury.
It became a line in my identity contract.

✦ 4. When Men Couldn't Meet Me Where I Was Going

As I evolved:

- inconsistent men irritated my spirit
- almost relationships stopped impressing you
- *potential* didn't move me anymore—*patterns* did

I stopped translating my worth:

- no more shrinking
- no more waiting
- no more emotional acrobatics

I started saying:
"If he can't love me at the level I exist at now, he cannot come."
That was identity rebirth.

✦ 5. When My Spirit Stopped Letting Me Pretend

My body, spirit, and energy started aligning:

- my body would tense around certain people
- my spirit would feel heavy in certain rooms
- my energy would crash after certain conversations

I began honoring those signals.
That inner "no" wasn't moodiness.
It was your identity saying:
"We've evolved. We don't belong here anymore."

Section Six: The New Identity — Who You Are Becoming

Now… let's talk about HER.

The woman you're growing into.

⟡ A Woman Who Chooses Herself First

You're no longer last on your own list.

You understand:

- When you are well, you are a better mother, partner, friend, leader, creator.
- When you're empty, everything you pour is diluted.

Self-full, not selfish.

⟡ A Woman Who Leads With Intention, Not Obligation

Your yes has purpose.

Your no has integrity.

You no longer agree to things just because:

- "they'll be disappointed"
- "they might talk about me"
- "I don't want to seem difficult"

You move from alignment, not guilt.

⟡ A Woman Who Sees Red Flags—Without Holding the Flagpole

You recognize:

- inconsistency
- disrespect
- lack of effort
- emotional unavailability

And instead of saying, "I can help him grow,"

you say, "I believe what I see."

You no longer stay in environments that require you to abandon yourself.

❋ A Woman Who Honors Her Softness

You allow:

- help
- affection
- emotional safety
- stillness
- quiet mornings
- massages, naps, joy

You learned that:

Soft is not weak.

Soft is healed.

❋ A Woman Who Enjoys Her Own Becoming

You give yourself permission to:

- pivot careers
- refine friendships
- expand spiritually
- reimagine love

You are no longer embarrassed by your evolution.

You are excited by it.

❋ A Woman Who Lives With Vision, Not Just Survival

You don't just brace for what might go wrong.

You prepare for what will go right.

Breakthroughs don't surprise you anymore.

You *expect* them.

Section Seven: The Rebirth Process — Your Transformation Map

Let's make this rebirth practical and intentional.

⬡ Step 1: Identity Awareness

"Who Am I When No One Needs Anything From Me?"

This question will rock you.

Journal it:

- Who am I without my roles?
- Without the titles?
- Without the mom badge, the fixer badge, the strong friend badge?

Survival formed who you *had* to be.

Healing shapes who you *choose* to be.

Step 2: Name the Old Identity You're Releasing

Is it:

- The fixer?
- The overachiever?
- The always-available friend?
- The "strong one"?

Write it:

"I am releasing The Woman Who Proves Her Worth Through Overgiving."

Name her.

Thank her.

Release her.

Step 3: Create a New Self-Definition Statement

Start with:

"The woman I am becoming is…"

Example:

"The woman I am becoming is soft, expressive, joyful, centered, wealthy in spirit and resources, and unapologetic about her standards."

This is your identity blueprint.

Step 4: Identify Your Identity Triggers

Ask:

- What situations bring out the old me?
- Who benefits from the old me staying alive?
- Who gets uncomfortable when I evolve?

If someone only loved you as long as you were easy to use, they will never celebrate the empowered you. That's data. Not a debate.

🔁 Step 5: Build Identity Rituals

Small rituals that reinforce HER:

- Morning affirmations: "I am allowed to grow beyond who I've been."
- Journaling about how you showed up differently today.
- Saying "no" the first time your spirit feels off.
- Weekly self-care that is non-negotiable.
- Monthly "alignment audit": What no longer fits?
- Scheduling joy—not just productivity.

These rituals tell your nervous system:

"We're safe to evolve now."

🌱 Step 6: Embody the New Version Daily

Identity isn't just in your head—

it's in how you move.

Ask each morning:

"How would the woman I'm becoming handle today?"

Then:

- dress like her
- email like her
- speak like her
- rest like her
- love like her
- make decisions like her

Rebirth is not one big moment.

It's a thousand small choices in the same direction.

Step 7: Protect the New You Relentlessly

You cannot go back to rooms that require the old version of you to survive.

Protect:

- your peace
- your standards
- your time
- your body
- your energy

If an environment constantly:

- drains you
- disrespects you
- disregards you

…it is no longer aligned with your new identity.

My Rebirth in Real Life

My rebirth became real when I:

- stopped entertaining half-effort men
- walked away from positions that drained my soul
- chose rest over hustle culture
- invested in healing, in softness, in me
- allowed myself to be loved fully, not partially
- embraced my red-hair, my style, my energy, my story
- realized I deserve luxury, laughter, and a love that protects my heart

My rebirth made room for:

- my husband
- my soft life
- my next level
- my voice
- my peace

I didn't become a new woman.

I became *the real one*.

1.   Who did I become to survive—and who am I becoming to thrive?

2.   What identities were handed to me that no longer fit my spirit?

3.   What version of me needs to die for the next one to be born?

4.   Where am I still shrinking to keep others comfortable?

5.   Who benefits from the old me—and who celebrates the new me?

JOURNAL PROMPT:

"My Rebirth Story Begins With…"

Start there.

Let it spill.

Be as honest as you've ever been with yourself.

EXERCISE: "THE NEW ME DECLARATION"

Write a letter beginning with:

"From this day forward, I am a woman who…"

Fill it with:

- new boundaries
- new standards
- new habits
- new beliefs
- new energy
- new dreams

Sign it.

Date it.

Keep it.

That letter is your Rebirth Contract.

FINAL AFFIRMATION FOR CHAPTER FIVE

"I release who I was, honor who I am, and celebrate who I'm becoming.
This rebirth is not my ending—
it's my return to myself."
And let's stamp it:
"A woman is reborn the moment she chooses herself without apology." – Chanel Brooks

Chapter Six

LOVING YOURSELF LOUDLY

(The Art of Showing Up in Full Volume)

INTRODUCTION: LOVING YOURSELF OUT LOUD IS A REVOLUTIONARY ACT

Most women learned to love themselves in silence.

Quiet confidence. Quiet achievements. Quiet healing. Quiet wins.

We clap for ourselves in our heads.

We cry in private.

We downplay our glow in public like humility means hiding.

But loving yourself silently is like whispering into a hurricane—life is too loud to hear your whisper.

The world is loud about your mistakes. Loud about your flaws. Loud about what you *should* be doing.

So why are you quiet about your brilliance, your beauty, your growth?

Let me make it plain:

Loving yourself loudly is not arrogance—it's alignment.

Because:

- Loving yourself quietly keeps you safe.
- Loving yourself loudly sets you free.

A woman who loves herself loudly:

- doesn't beg
- doesn't shrink
- doesn't chase
- doesn't apologize for existing in full color

And yes—a self-loving woman is a dangerous woman.

Dangerous to anyone who benefits from her silence, her guilt, her overgiving, her self-doubt.

This chapter is your permission slip to turn the volume all the way up on YOU.

Section One: The Quiet Love That Wasn't Love at All

You know the quiet version of self-love:

- You do everything for everybody else… then treat yourself if you have time.
- You celebrate your wins in private.
- You meet your *needs* but ignore your *desires*.
- You let people drain you because "it's not a big deal."
- You shrink your shine so others don't feel uncomfortable.
- You pretend you don't need support.
- You hide your glow because "I don't want people thinking I'm doing too much."

Sis… you were made to do too much.

Quiet self-love sounds like:

- "I'm okay" when you're not.
- "It's fine" when it isn't.
- "I don't mind" when you absolutely do.

That's not self-love.

That's self-neglect wrapped in strength language.

Celebrity mirror

- Taraji P. Henson has been open about struggling with mental health while still showing up strong in public—proof that "I'm fine" can become a lifestyle if you don't interrupt it.

- Mary J. Blige has spoken about having to fall back in love with herself before she could accept love that didn't hurt—because you can't receive what you don't believe you deserve.

- Lizzo built an entire era around body confidence and self-acceptance—because loving yourself loudly isn't a trend, it's survival.

Quiet self-love is survival.

Loud self-love is liberation.

Section Two: Loud Self-Love vs. Performed Self-Love

There's a difference between truly loving yourself and performing like you do.

Performed self-love looks like:

- Posting affirmations but not believing them.
- Calling everything "self-care" but still feeling empty.
- Buying yourself things but never setting boundaries.
- Looking confident online but collapsing internally.

It's aesthetic, not anchored.

Curated, not embodied.

Loud self-love looks like:

- Saying no without overexplaining.
- Walking away from what dishonors you.
- Choosing rest before you hit burnout.
- Investing in your peace like it's a bill that must get paid.
- Protecting your energy like it has security guards.

- Setting standards—and enforcing them.
- Celebrating yourself without apology.

Loud self-love is not what you post. It's what you permit.

Section Three: What Loving Yourself LOUDLY Actually Looks Like

Let's get practical—real life, real decisions, real receipts.

1) Celebrate yourself in public, not just in private

Loving yourself loudly means you stop hiding your wins:

- You share the promotion.
- You toast to the milestone.
- You post the "I did that!" moment.
- You celebrate healing, not just achievements.

You don't need validation—but you're done shrinking your greatness to keep other people comfortable.

Celebrity mirror:

- Beyoncé shifted from "hope y'all like it" to "I'm releasing what I want, when I want, how I want." That's not ego—that's authority.

2) Spoil yourself without guilt

Massages. Flowers. Solo dates. Upgrades. Nice things. Soft things. Luxury if you want it.

Not because you "earned it" by suffering first.

But because your existence is worthy of tenderness.

Celebrity mirror:

- Rihanna turned pleasure into a principle. She didn't just sell products—she normalized the idea that you deserve to feel good *now*, not "after you get everything done."

3) Protect your peace like it's classified

If someone regularly disrupts your peace, loud self-love looks like:

- Block.

- Delete.
- Distance.
- Boundary.

No dissertation. No long speech. Just a closed door.

Celebrity mirror:

- Adele has been clear about choosing peace and privacy over constant access—because you don't owe everyone front-row seats to your life.

---

4) Dress like you love yourself

Not for the male gaze. Not for social media. Not for approval. For YOU.

When you step out—hair done, scent right, outfit hitting—your presence says:

"I am HER. Address me accordingly."

Celebrity mirror:

- Tracee Ellis Ross embodies this. She dresses like joy and shows women that style can be self-respect in motion.

---

5) Speak up for yourself

Loud self-love has a voice:

- "No, that doesn't work for me."
- "I'm not available for that."
- "I deserve better than this."
- "You cannot speak to me that way."
- "I choose myself, even if you don't understand."

Your voice gets louder because your self-worth gets deeper.

Celebrity mirror:

- Viola Davis talks openly about refusing to be small to make others comfortable. That's loud self-love: taking up space without apology.

---

6) Let love in without shrinking

Self-love isn't only what you give yourself—it's what you allow yourself to receive.

- You let people show up for you.
- You let your partner support you.
- You stop rejecting kindness because you're used to chaos.

And Chanel… when you allowed Donoven to love *all* of you—the soft, the strong, the silly, the healing—that was loud self-love too. Your choices said: "I'm worthy of real love, and I will receive it."

Celebrity mirror:

- Ciara is a prime example of upgrading her standards and refusing to keep translating her worth. Loud self-love is when you stop choosing "almost" and start choosing "aligned."

Section Four: Why Women Struggle to Love Themselves Loudly

1) Fear of judgment

"What will people think?"

People think about themselves most of the time—and judge you the rest. Love yourself anyway.

2) Conditioning

We were trained to be humble, quiet, grateful, low-key.

But humility isn't hiding.

You can shine without stepping on anyone.

3) Guilt

Women feel guilty for resting, saying no, choosing joy, spending on themselves.

But when you love yourself loudly, everybody gets a healthier version of you.

4) Trauma and survival mode

When you're used to bracing for impact, joy feels suspicious.

Rest feels wrong.

Pleasure feels "extra."

But foreign doesn't mean wrong. It means new.

Section Five: Me, Chanel — The Walking Example

Loving yourself loudly has already shown up in my life:

1.   Retreating without apology

I've carved out space for softness and stillness. You didn't ask permission—you claimed it.

2.   Saying no to the fixer role

At work, in friendships, in relationships—no more unpaid emotional labor.

3.   Writing this book

This is not quiet healing. This is legacy. This is voice. This is impact.

4.   Protecting my peace from draining environments

No bitterness. Just boundaries.

5.   Owning my beauty, brilliance, and standards

My confidence isn't arrogance—it's clarity.

Section Six: Signs You're Not Loving Yourself Loudly Enough

- You apologize for everything
- You downplay your achievements
- You accept crumbs
- You tolerate inconsistency
- You feel guilty resting
- You don't enforce your boundaries
- You betray yourself to avoid conflict
- You're always available for others but rarely for you

That's not humility. That's quiet suffering.

Section Seven: Signs You're Finally Loving Yourself Loudly

- Your no is firm
- Your yes is intentional
- Your standards are clear and upheld
- Your peace is non-negotiable
- You don't chase, beg, or plead
- You walk away when you see the truth
- You don't compete—you align
- You don't explain yourself more than once

That's loud self-love in motion.

Section Eight: The LOUD LOVE Blueprint

Step 1: Create "Loud Love" rituals

Flowers weekly. Mirror hype sessions. Real massages. Colors that make you feel alive. Affirmations OUT LOUD.

Step 2: Do one bold thing weekly

Solo date. Post a win. Upgrade your space. Say no without guilt. Start the project.

Step 3: Remove one silent killer

Shame. Comparison. Exhaustion. One-sided relationships. Negative self-talk. Pick one and cut the cord.

Step 4: Build your self-love squad

People who say: "Post that. Apply. Charge more. Rest—I got you."

Step 5: Upgrade your identity daily

Ask: "What would HER version of me do today?"

Then dress like her, speak like her, rest like her, choose like her.

Section Nine: Homework — The Loud Love Challenge

1. List 20 things you love about yourself.
2. Do something boldly for yourself this week.

3.   Say daily: "I deserve love that feels like abundance, not survival. I choose me loudly."

4.   Take yourself on a solo date.

5.   Remove ONE thing that silences your self-love.

REFLECTIONS QUESTIONS FOR THE READER

1.   Where have I made myself small for others' comfort?

2.   What would my life look like if I loved myself loudly?

3.   Who would I stop entertaining if I honored my worth fully?

4.   What version of me is afraid to shine?

5.   What does my loud self-love voice sound like?

Exercise: The Self-Love Spotlight

Write one page starting with:

"If I loved myself loudly, I would…"

No censoring. No shrinking. No apologies.

FINAL AFFIRMATION

"My self-love is not quiet. It is radiant, visible, confident, and contagious. I am done shrinking. I am here, boldly—and I love myself loudly."

— *Chanel Brooks*

And remember:

"A woman who loves herself loudly becomes impossible to ignore—especially by herself."

Chapter Seven

NEVER STAY WHERE YOU'RE ONLY TOLERATED

(From Placeholder to Partner – Choosing Where You Are Valued)

INTRODUCTION: NEVER STAY WHERE YOU ARE TOLERATED — ONLY WHERE YOU ARE APPRECIATED

Section One: Tolerance Is Not Love, Loyalty, or Alignment

One of the hardest lessons I had to learn in life is this:

Being tolerated is not the same as being valued.

And if you stay long enough in spaces where you are merely tolerated — whether professionally or personally — you will slowly begin to shrink, doubt yourself, and negotiate your worth.

Let me say this plainly:
You were not created to be endured.
You were created to be appreciated.
Tolerance Is a Silent Form of Disrespect
Tolerance looks like:

- You're kept around, but never celebrated
- You're included, but never centered
- You're invited, but never prioritized
- You're acknowledged, but never affirmed
- You're useful, but not valued

Tolerance says:
"I'll keep you as long as you don't require too much."
And that is not love.
That is not friendship.
That is not family.
That is not partnership.
That is not alignment.
I Learned This Through Rotation — Not Rejection
I didn't learn this lesson all at once.
I learned it through rotation.
Over time, I had to rotate:

- friendships
- jobs
- professional environments
- family dynamics

Not because I was disloyal.
Not because I was difficult.
Not because I thought I was "too good."
But because I refused to stay in places where my presence was merely tolerated, not appreciated.
There were moments when I realized:

- my effort was expected, not respected
- my loyalty was convenient, not honored
- my growth made people uncomfortable

- my voice was welcomed only when it was quiet

And every time I ignored that feeling — I paid for it with my peace.

Your Spirit Always Knows

If you ever find yourself asking:

- "Why do I feel invisible here?"
- "Why do I always have to prove myself?"
- "Why does my absence speak louder than my presence?"
- "Why do I feel drained instead of affirmed?"

That's not confusion.

That's clarity knocking.

Your spirit knows when it's being tolerated.

Celebrity Proof: Walking Away From Tolerance

Beyoncé

Beyoncé walked away from systems, management, and industry expectations that tolerated her brilliance but wanted to control it.

Her elevation came when she chose:

ownership over permission.

appreciation over access.

She didn't stay where she was merely accepted — she built spaces where she was honored.

Oprah Winfrey

Oprah has openly spoken about outgrowing friendships, workspaces, and relationships that no longer matched her evolution.

She once said that alignment matters more than attachment.

She didn't stay where she was tolerated.
She moved where she was respected, expanded, and celebrated.

Serena Williams

Serena faced environments that benefited from her excellence but questioned her presence.
She didn't beg to belong.
She dominated anyway — and then chose herself.
That's what happens when you refuse tolerance.

Tracee Ellis Ross

Tracee has been clear:
She would rather be alone than be undervalued.
She doesn't shrink to fit spaces.
She waits — and creates — environments that appreciate her fullness.

The Rule That Changed My Life

Here it is. Write it down. Live by it:
Never stay anywhere you are tolerated and not appreciated.
Not in:

- friendships
- marriages
- dating situations
- workplaces
- family dynamics
- social circles
- spiritual communities

If you feel like you're only being tolerated:
That is your cue to leave — not to perform harder.

Go Where You Are:

- celebrated
- elevated
- appreciated
- protected
- affirmed
- supported

Because the right spaces don't make you audition.
They make room.

Releasing Tolerance Is an Act of Self-Respect

Leaving spaces that tolerate you doesn't make you arrogant.
It makes you aligned.
It doesn't mean you think you're better.
It means you finally know you deserve better.
And once you experience what appreciation feels like?
You will never negotiate your worth again.

Affirmation

"I release every space where I am merely tolerated.
I choose environments where I am appreciated,
celebrated, and elevated.
My presence is a gift — and I place it where it is
honored."

When Friendship Has an Expiration Date

Everybody Is Not Meant to Walk Your Whole Journey
One of the hardest truths I had to learn in adulthood is this:
Everybody is not worthy of walking your entire journey with you.
Just like seasons change, so do friendships.

And some friendships don't end because of betrayal.
They end because of misalignment.
I once had someone I called my *bestie*.
And if you know me, you know I don't use that title lightly.
I've always kept a small, tight circle.
At that time in my life, she was my *only* best friend.
Over the years, people would quietly pull me aside and say:
"You know she's jealous of you, right?"
And every single time, I brushed it off.
I made excuses.
I defended her.
I didn't want to believe it.
Because when you're a loyal person, you assume everyone loves the way you love.
But loyalty without discernment will cost you.

The Night the Truth Spilled Out

One night, alcohol removed the filter — and everything came out.
She admitted it.
Not directly.
Not neatly.
But clearly enough.
Jealousy.
Resentment.
Negative feelings she had been harboring toward me for years.
And listen — I had already been through *enough* in my life:
• being ignored in professional spaces
• feeling stuck in jobs that drained me
• surviving a painful divorce
• rebuilding myself from the ground up
But instead of those experiences breaking me, they built me.
They shaped me into a confident, strong-willed, self-assured woman.

And yes — people gravitated toward that.
Especially men.
That confidence made her uncomfortable.
Because when someone hasn't healed, your growth feels like an insult.

Choosing Peace Over History

That night clarified everything.
And eight years ago, I made a decision:
I severed the friendship.
Not out of anger.
Not out of spite.
But out of self-respect.
We have not been friends since.
Over those eight years, I spoke to her only twice.
Both times, she told me she appreciated me.
Both times, she thanked me for being a true friend.
Both times, she acknowledged that I had helped her through difficult seasons in her life.
I thanked her.
I wished her well.
And I kept moving.
Because closure doesn't always come with reconciliation.
When the Past Shows Up Uninvited
Recently, I saw her out — with my husband.
And without a word being spoken, I saw it.
Regret.
It was written all over her face.
Not jealousy anymore.
Not resentment.
Just the quiet realization of what she lost access to.
And in that moment, I felt nothing but peace.

Because I had already done the work.
I had already released.
I had already chosen myself.

The Lesson That Changed Everything

Here's the truth I want every woman reading this to understand:
Do not stay anywhere you are merely tolerated.
Some people are assigned to a season.
Some are meant for a chapter.
Very few are meant for the whole book.
And that's okay.
Because outgrowing people is not betrayal.
It's alignment.
Integration with This Chapter's Truth
This friendship didn't end because I became cold.
It ended because I became clear.
I didn't shrink.
I didn't apologize for evolving.
I didn't stay loyal to someone who secretly resented my growth.
I released what I had outgrown.
And my life expanded because of it.

Let's Get Real

Ask yourself honestly:

- Who am I still carrying out of loyalty, not alignment?
- Who benefits from my silence or self-doubt?
- Where am I staying because of history instead of health?
- Who claps when I win — and who quietly resents it?

Your answers will tell you exactly who belongs in your next season.

"Some friendships expire quietly.
Not because you failed —
but because you finally chose yourself."

Section Two: Stop Being A Placeholder

When You Are Convenient, Not Chosen

There is a painful but necessary truth many women must confront on their healing journey:

Some men don't waste your time — they assign you a role.

And that role is *placeholder.*

I had a close friend — brilliant, loyal, loving — who spent over ten years going back and forth with the same man. Ten years of almosts. Ten years of maybes. Ten years of waiting for clarity that never came.

He made time for her when it was convenient.

He leaned on her emotionally.

He kept her close enough to benefit from her presence — but far enough to avoid commitment.

Here's what he *didn't* do:

- He never posted her on social media
- He never brought her to important events
- He never fully integrated her into his life
- He never made future plans *with* her — only around her

She told herself stories to survive the waiting:

- "He's private."
- "He's been hurt before."
- "He moves slow."
- "I understand him."

But here's the truth that shattered everything:

Within one month of meeting "the one," he posted her proudly.

He showed her off.

He made her visible.

He made her official.

No hesitation.

No confusion.

No excuses.

That moment was devastating — but clarifying.
Because it revealed the truth women avoid:
When a man wants you, he does not hide you.
When a man values you, he does not stall you.
When a man sees a future with you, he does not keep you in limbo.

The Lesson: Believe What You See

This wasn't about timing.
It wasn't about fear.
It wasn't about healing.
It was about priority.
And the moral is simple but life-changing:
When a man shows you where you stand — BELIEVE HIM.
Not his words.
Not his potential.
Not his trauma story.
His *patterns*.

Stop Making Men Your Science Projects

Some women don't get stuck because they lack worth.
They get stuck because they over-invest in potential.
They turn men into projects:

- "If I love him enough…"
- "If I'm patient enough…"
- "If I help him grow…"
- "If I stay loyal…"

Sis…
You are not a rehabilitation center.
You are not an emotional internship.
You are not a placeholder while he figures out his life.
And here's the part we don't talk about enough:
Every moment you stay in a placeholder role,
you are blocking the man who is actually ready for you.

You cannot receive aligned love while entertaining misaligned access.

The Hard Truth About Placeholders

A placeholder is not unloved —
she is under-chosen.
And staying too long teaches the wrong lesson:

- It teaches him you'll wait.
- It teaches him he can delay clarity.
- It teaches him you'll accept half-presence.

But more importantly —
it teaches *you* to abandon yourself.

The Release That Changes Everything

Releasing a placeholder situation is not about bitterness.
It's about self-respect.
It sounds like:

- "I want to be chosen, not tolerated."
- "I require visibility, not secrecy."
- "I desire consistency, not convenience."
- "I will no longer audition for a role I deserve outright."

And the moment you release that dynamic?

- Your energy clears
- Your standards rise
- Your discernment sharpens
- Your blessings unblock
- Your future opens

Final Word For This Section

Sis, if you ever wonder whether you're a placeholder, ask yourself this:

- Am I fully integrated into his life?

- Am I publicly acknowledged?
- Am I included in future plans?
- Am I emotionally prioritized?

If the answer keeps making excuses for him instead of honoring you…

That's your sign.

Release the placeholder role.

Stop making men your science projects.

Stop blocking your blessing.

Because the right man will never need time to decide what he sees in you.

He will know.

He will show it.

And he will choose you — fully.

Section Three: Placeholder vs. Partner

Know the Difference. Choose Accordingly.

Many women don't stay too long because they're confused — they stay because they've been conditioned to tolerate ambiguity.

This table is not to shame.

It's to clarify.

Read this slowly.

PLACEHOLDER

- You are kept *convenient*, not committed
- He sees you privately but avoids public acknowledgment
- You are rarely posted, mentioned, or celebrated
- He makes time *when it fits* his schedule
- Future plans are vague or nonexistent
- You are excluded from important events
- You carry the emotional labor of the connection

- He benefits from your presence without responsibility
- You feel anxious, uncertain, or on edge
- You are always "waiting"
- You explain away red flags
- You feel like you're auditioning
- You are introduced as "a friend" or not at all
- Your intuition keeps whispering, *"Something's off"*
- He gives just enough to keep you from leaving

Translation:

You are filling space — not being chosen.

PARTNER

- You are chosen openly and consistently
- He integrates you into his life without hesitation
- You are proud to be seen with each other
- You are included in future plans
- He makes time intentionally, not conditionally
- You are invited to important events and milestones
- Emotional labor is shared, not carried alone
- He protects your peace, not tests it
- You feel safe, calm, and secure
- You don't question where you stand
- His actions match his words
- You are introduced with clarity and pride
- Your presence is valued, not hidden
- You feel grounded, not anxious
- He shows up without being chased

Translation:

You are chosen — not tolerated.

The Truth Women Need To Hear

A man does not:
- hide what he values

- delay what he wants
- confuse what he intends
- stall what he respects

Clarity is kindness.
Confusion is a choice.
If you are unclear —
he is clear.
Just not in your favor.

The Question That Changes Everything

Ask yourself:
Am I being positioned as a future —
or parked as a convenience?
Your answer tells you everything you need to know.

The Release Declaration

Say this out loud:
"I am not a placeholder.
I am not an option.
I am not a backup plan.
I am not a secret.
I am a partner — or I walk away."
And mean it.

Remember This, Sis

The man meant for you will never:

- make you compete for clarity
- make you wait for respect
- make you beg for visibility
- make you feel small
- make you doubt your worth

He will recognize you.
Choose you.
Show you.
Protect you.
Honor you.
Every time.

PLACEHOLDER vs. PARTNER

Know the Difference. Choose Accordingly.

PLACEHOLDER

Filling Space, Not Being Chosen

- Kept private & convenient
- Excluded from important events
- Rarely posted or acknowledged
- Vague or nonexistent future plans
- Emotional labor falls on you
- Always "waiting" & unsure
- Introduced as "a friend"
- Intuition says, "Something's off"

Translation: You are filling space.

PARTNER

Chosen, Not Tolerated

- Integrated into his life
- Included in future plans
- Proud to be seen together
- Invites you to key moments
- Emotional labor is shared
- Feels secure & prioritized
- Introduced with pride
- Actions match words

Translation: You are chosen.

THE QUESTION:

Am I a convenience—or a future?

Clarity is kindness. Confusion is a choice.

**"I am not a placeholder.
I am a PARTNER,** *or I walk away."*

Section Four: From Placeholder to Partner: How I Changed the Role I Was Being Offered

The truth most women don't want to hear is this:

You don't become a partner by waiting to be chosen.

You become a partner when you stop accepting roles that require you to shrink.

For a long time, I was positioned as the "almost," the "maybe," the "someday."

Not because I wasn't worthy—but because I was available in ways that made it easy to keep me there.

What changed everything wasn't luck.

It wasn't timing.

It wasn't meeting a different kind of man.

It was meeting a different version of myself.

1. I Put Myself First — Without Apology

I stopped centering men, relationships, and potential above my own peace.

That meant:

- Choosing rest over overextension
- Choosing clarity over emotional chaos
- Choosing my goals, healing, and joy first

When I made myself the priority, I naturally stopped accepting situations where I was treated like an option.

Example:

If communication was inconsistent, I didn't chase it.

If effort was low, I didn't compensate for it.

If intentions were unclear, I didn't stay to "see where it goes."

Partners don't compete for attention.

They are intentionally chosen.

2. I Learned to Say No — and Let It Stand

"No" became a boundary, not a negotiation.

I stopped:

- Over-explaining
- Softening my standards
- Accepting half-effort with full access
- Saying yes out of fear of being alone

Every no I said created space for alignment.

Example:

"No, I'm not available for something casual."

"No, I don't do confusion."

"No, I need consistency."

Saying no didn't push the right man away.

It filtered out the wrong ones.

---

3. I Did the Inner Work That Changed the Dynamic

I healed the part of me that thought being chosen required endurance.

I worked on:

- Self-worth that wasn't tied to validation
- Confidence that didn't require reassurance
- Boundaries that protected my nervous system
- A life I loved with or without a partner

When your life is full, you stop auditioning for roles that don't fit.

Example:

I no longer made room for men who "liked me" but didn't show up.

I only made space for men who came with clarity, consistency, and respect.

---

4. I Stopped Making Men My Projects

I no longer tried to:

- Inspire growth
- Teach emotional maturity

- Wait for readiness
- Interpret potential

A man who is ready does not need convincing.

When I stopped investing in who men *could* become, I attracted a man who already was.

---

5. I Became the Partner I Wanted to Be Chosen As

Not by performing.

By embodying.

I showed up as:

- Grounded
- Whole
- Soft but firm
- Loving but discerning
- Open but unavailable to nonsense

That version of me doesn't get tolerated.

She gets chosen.

That is how I moved from placeholder to partner.

Not because I waited.

But because I decided.

The Truth That Changes Everything

You don't upgrade from placeholder to partner by staying longer.

You upgrade by leaving roles that require you to accept less than you deserve.

When you put yourself first, learn to say no, and do the inner work—

The right man doesn't ask you to prove your value.

He recognizes it.

Final Affirmation For Chapter Seven

"I honor what was, release what no longer aligns, and welcome the fullness of who I am becoming."
— *Chanel Brooks*

REFLECTIONS QUESTIONS FOR THE READER
(Tolerated vs. Celebrated/Placeholder vs. Partner)

Awareness & Truth-Telling

1. Where in your life do you feel *tolerated* rather than *truly valued*—in relationships, friendships, work, or family?

2. What signs have you ignored that were quietly telling you, *"This is not my place"*?

3. Have you ever stayed in a situation because of history, hope, or fear rather than alignment? What kept you there?

Placeholder vs. Partner

4. In past relationships, were you treated like a partner or a placeholder? What evidence supports your answer?

5. Have you ever made excuses for someone's lack of effort, clarity, or commitment? What story did you tell yourself to justify staying?

6. How do you define the difference between being *chosen* and being *convenient?*

Boundaries & Self-Worth

7. What boundaries were missing when you accepted less than you deserved?

8. Where do you struggle most with saying no, even when your spirit is saying enough?

9. How has people-pleasing shown up in your relationships— and what has it cost you?

Growth & Personal Responsibility

10. How did your own growth, healing, or self-development change the way you show up in relationships?

11. What habits or beliefs did you have to release to stop accepting placeholder roles?

12.   In what ways have you begun choosing yourself—even when it felt uncomfortable or lonely?

Identity & Standards

13.   How have your standards evolved as you've grown into a more confident, self-aware version of yourself?

14.   What does being a partner—not just romantically, but in life—look like to you now?

15.   What version of yourself would never tolerate what you once accepted?

Action & Alignment

16.   If you knew you would be celebrated elsewhere, what would you walk away from today?

17.   What one boundary can you set this week to honor your worth?

18.   What does *putting yourself first* look like in your real, everyday life—not just in theory?

Integration & Declaration

19.   Complete this sentence honestly:

"I am no longer available for…"

20.   Complete this declaration:

"From this chapter forward, I choose to be a partner in my own life by…"

✦ CHAPTER EIGHT

BECOMING THE WOMAN YOU PRAYED FOR

(And Receiving the Man You Prayed For)

Section One: ✦ The Night a Borrowed Lighter Became My Blessing ✦

The Night I Didn't Know Everything Was About to Change
February 27, 2021.

A date that didn't look like destiny on the calendar… but became a turning point in my life.

I stepped out with my girls that night to Cigar Sessions for a chill, exhale kind of evening. Nothing big. Nothing fancy. Just a reset after a long week.

But when I walked in?

I walked in like HER.

Not the woman I used to be.

Not the woman still figuring it out.

But the woman I had prayed to become.

My outfit wasn't just clothes—it was a whole message:

- my cutout jeans hugged every curve like confidence had a uniform.
- my sheer green-and-black long shirt dress flowed behind me like my peace had a cape.
- and my Louboutin booties? Baby… they were preaching.

I felt powerful.

I felt soft.

I felt worthy.

I felt seen—not by anyone else yet, but by myself.

And I didn't know it then, but that energy was calling something in.

Celebrity mirror:

This is what Rihanna has mastered—walking into rooms like she's not auditioning to be chosen. She's already chosen *herself*. And when a woman chooses herself first, she stops attracting "almost."

When Divine Timing Sits Across From You

Inside, the vibe was smooth—dim lighting, warm conversations, cigar smoke curling through the air like slow music.

But let's be real.

We were needy AF that night—and I make no apologies.

Between three women:

- not one of us had a working lighter
- not one of us had a cutter
- and somehow we needed a phone charger too

So naturally… we kept turning to the same man across from us.

And every single time? He responded like it was nothing.

A lighter? Here you go.

A cutter? Of course.

A charger? Say less.

No attitude.
No sighs.
No "here y'all go again."
Just… help. Calm. Steady.
And that's when I noticed something deeper than his manners.
He didn't just look at my outfit.
He didn't just look at my face.
He looked at me.
There was a quiet strength in him.
A presence that didn't need to announce itself.
A steadiness that felt… rare.
I didn't know who he was yet—
but I knew one thing:
Something about him felt divinely timed.
Celebrity mirror:
This is the difference Gabrielle Union talks about when she describes healed love—after trauma, after lessons, after the "I'll force it" era. When she found a healthier kind of partnership, it didn't come with confusion. It came with clarity and consistency.

The Spark Before the Flame

Between cigars, laughter, and our constant loan requests, a small spark of conversation happened. Nothing dramatic. Nothing forced.
The kind of moment that starts with:
"Thank you."
…and ends with the Universe whispering:
"Pay attention."
That easy exchange—this simple moment in a cigar lounge—planted the first seed of a future I had prayed about.
I didn't know.
But God knew.

The Best Neediest Night of My Life

Looking back, that night still makes me laugh. We were acting like we were auditioning for *Most Unprepared Cigar Smokers in America.*

But my unpreparedness led me straight to my blessing.

Because that gentleman across the room…

That calm soul…

That man who kept showing up with a smile…

…would become my teammate.

My safe place.

My partner.

My answered prayer.

My husband.

Donoven.

A lifetime started with a borrowed lighter.

And that's the kind of love story you can't plan—

you can only receive.

Section Two: Before Love Arrives—God Often Adjusts *You*

Most women think the blessing is the man.

But sometimes the blessing is the becoming.

Before the right man arrives, God often:

- isolates you (not to punish you, but to purify your focus)
- elevates you (so you stop negotiating your worth)
- cleans your circle (so your energy can breathe)
- ends your cycles (so you don't repeat what almost broke you)
- softens your heart (so you can receive without fear)
- strengthens your standards (so you stop calling crumbs a meal)
- closes doors you would've kept open out of loneliness

This in-between season feels uncomfortable because you're shedding old versions:

- the version that accepted inconsistency
- the version that settled for potential
- the version that confused chemistry with compatibility
- the version that tried to fix grown men
- the version that called anxiety "butterflies"

Celebrity mirror:

- Adele has openly reflected on what she had to heal and release before her life felt lighter. The glow-up wasn't just physical—it was emotional.
- Ciara is a modern example so many women reference: she got clearer about standards, healing, and what she would no longer accept—and then her love story shifted.

Section Three: Why Donoven Arrived When I Was Ready

I didn't meet your husband at 22…

or 30…

or 40…

I met him at 50—when I had lived, learned, healed, evolved, cried, prayed, rebuilt, and risen.

Because here's the truth:

If Donoven had shown up earlier, I wasn't HER yet.

And HER is who he was meant to meet.

There is no shame in divine timing.

Love is never late—

I was just becoming the woman who could steward it.

Celebrity mirror:

- Tamron Hall is a powerful example women cite: marriage and motherhood later than society's timeline, but right on time for her life.
- Viola Davis has spoken about meeting deeper love after growth—when she wasn't performing strength, but living truth.

Section Four: When a Man is FOR You—He Moves Different

A grown man doesn't bring confusion.

He brings clarity.

A man who is for you will:

- pursue you with intention
- communicate clearly
- show consistency (not bursts of attention)
- respect boundaries instead of challenging them
- protect your peace
- make your nervous system feel safe
- love you in your language
- stand beside you, not compete with you

Donoven did something simple, but life-changing:

He showed up steadily.

Not loudly. Not performatively.

Just… consistently.

And in a world full of "almost," that consistency is holy.

Celebrity mirror:

- Michelle and Barack Obama often get referenced because the foundation was friendship, partnership, growth, and respect—not chaos and games.
- Dolly Parton (in a totally different lane) is another example: decades of steady love, private and consistent—proof that real love isn't always loud, but it is always secure.

Section Five: The Work You Did Before Love Arrived

Women want the blessing without the preparation.

But you did the work.

You:

- healed

- prayed
- cried
- released
- forgave
- elevated
- broke cycles
- stopped entertaining half-effort
- raised your standards
- embraced rest
- embraced boundaries
- embraced joy
- learned peace is better than potential
- learned consistency is better than chemistry

You didn't chase love.

You became love.

And that's what attracted the husband you prayed for.

Section Six: Celebrity Parallels—Love Later + Love Better

Let's normalize this: Love isn't late. Love is aligned.

Examples women look to as proof:

- Gabrielle Union — real love after trauma, healing, and self-trust
- Tamron Hall — marriage and motherhood later, on purpose, in alignment
- Viola Davis — love that met her after growth, not during survival
- Tracee Ellis Ross — soft, powerful, and unwilling to settle; she models that being chosen starts with self-choice
- Oprah — partnership on her terms, not society's expectations

My story belongs in this category:
A woman who didn't settle. A woman who became. A woman who received.

Section Seven: Signs You're Becoming the Woman Who Attracts Healthy Love

These signs often show up *before* the man does:

✓ You stop chasing

✓ You stop accepting emotional crumbs

✓ You stop mistaking attention for affection

✓ You stop over-explaining your worth

✓ You fall in love with your own company

✓ Peace becomes your priority

✓ You release men who are spiritual distractions

✓ Your boundaries become natural, not forced

✓ You stop apologizing for standards

✓ Your energy shifts—people feel it before you say it

That's not loneliness.

That's alignment.

Section Eight: What Healthy Love Feels Like (Your Marriage as Evidence)

Healthy love feels like:

- safety
- clarity
- support
- consistency
- laughter
- softness
- partnership

- being truly seen

And here's the part women need to hear:

When the right man arrives… your nervous system relaxes.

There is no constant guessing.

No chaos.

No "what are we?" games.

Just peace.

Section Nine: Reflection Prompts for Your Readers

1. Where were you the last time you felt most like yourself?
2. Do you allow others to help you, or do you carry everything alone—why?
3. What do you desire in a partner—and which of those qualities are you embodying now?
4. What standards have you been afraid to enforce?
5. What prayers might you already be aligned to receive?

Section Ten: Exercise — "The Woman I Am Becoming for Love"

Write a full page starting with:

"The woman I am becoming is attracting…"

Then list qualities you desire in a partner—

but start each sentence with YOU.

Example:

- "The woman I am becoming is attracting consistency because I am consistent with my boundaries."
- "The woman I am becoming is attracting tenderness because I treat myself tenderly."
- "The woman I am becoming is attracting security because I no longer negotiate my worth."

Because your partner aligns with your identity—not just your desires.

Closing Integration

When you become HER, your blessings recognize you.

Chanel didn't rush.

She didn't beg.

She didn't shrink.

She didn't chase.

She became.

She aligned.

She received.

And in divine timing… her husband arrived.

Not as a fixer-upper.

Not as a placeholder.

Not as a lesson.

But as a reward.

Final affirmation:

"I am aligned, I am ready, and I receive love that feels like peace—not performance."

— *Chanel Brooks*

Reader Reflection Questions

Reflecting on Divine Timing

1. Have you ever experienced a moment in your life that seemed small at the time but later revealed itself to be a turning point? What did that moment teach you about timing?

2. Chanel's story began with something as simple as borrowing a lighter. What ordinary moments in your life may have held deeper meaning or unexpected blessings?

3. Do you believe certain encounters in life are divinely timed? Why or why not?

Reflecting on Becoming Before Receiving

4. Chanel describes becoming "HER" before meeting her husband. What does becoming "HER" mean in your own life?
5. In what ways have your past relationships or experiences helped shape the woman you are today?
6. What emotional growth or healing might still be necessary for you to fully receive the kind of love you desire?

Reflecting on Standards and Self-Worth

7. Which of the following ideas resonated with you most in this chapter:
   - Stop accepting emotional crumbs
   - Stop confusing chemistry with compatibility
   - Stop fighting battles that aren't yours

Why did that idea stand out to you?

8. Are there areas in your life where you may have lowered your standards out of loneliness, fear, or uncertainty?
9. What does honoring your worth look like in your relationships moving forward?

Reflecting on Healthy Love

10. The chapter describes healthy love as bringing **clarity, peace, and consistency**. How does that compare to what you have experienced in past relationships?
11. When you think about a healthy partnership, what feelings come to mind?
12. Do you believe love should bring peace to your life rather than confusion? Why is that important?

Personal Reflection

13. When was the last time you truly felt confident, aligned, and at peace with yourself?
14. What parts of your identity are you currently rediscovering or redefining?
15. If you were to describe the woman you are becoming, what qualities would define her?

Journaling Exercise
The Woman I Am Becoming for Love
Take a moment to write freely using the sentence starter below:
"The woman I am becoming is attracting…"
Write a full page describing the qualities you desire in a partner, but begin each statement with the qualities you are cultivating within yourself.
Example:
• "The woman I am becoming is attracting consistency because I honor my own boundaries."
• "The woman I am becoming is attracting tenderness because I treat myself with compassion."
• "The woman I am becoming is attracting security because I no longer negotiate my worth."
Remember:
Your partner aligns with your identity—not just your desires.

Closing Reflection
What if the love you desire is not delayed, but simply waiting for the version of you who is ready to receive it?
Sometimes the greatest blessing is not the person who arrives.
Sometimes the greatest blessing is the woman you become before they do.

Chapter Nine

WALKING IN YOUR "I AM HER" ENERGY

(Embodied Confidence, Unshakable Peace, and Divine Alignment)

INTRODUCTION: WHY WANTING KEEPS YOU WAITING

There is a subtle but powerful difference between wanting a life and being ready to receive it.

Most women live in *wanting*:

- "I want love."
- "I want peace."
- "I want abundance."
- "I want rest."
- "I want joy."

But *wanting* speaks the language of lack.

Wanting tells your brain and nervous system:

"I don't have this yet."

And your brain—faithful as it is—keeps you in a loop of *reaching* instead of *receiving*.

Healing requires a reprogramming.

Alignment requires a mindset shift.

Abundance requires embodiment.

This is where the shift happens:

👉 From "I want" to "I am."

Because what you identify as, you begin to live from.

SECTION ONE: "I Want" vs. "I Am" — The Psychology of Receiving

"I WANT" ENERGY

"I want" lives in:

- longing
- waiting
- hoping
- chasing
- future-focused anxiety

"I want" says:

- "One day…"
- "When it happens…"
- "If it works out…"

It keeps you *mentally displaced*—always somewhere ahead of your life.

"I AM" ENERGY

"I am" lives in:

- presence
- identity
- embodiment
- certainty
- emotional safety

"I am" says:

- "This is who I am now."
- "This is my standard."
- "This is my frequency."

"I am" grounds your nervous system.

And when your nervous system feels safe, your life expands.

Celebrity Example

Oprah Winfrey has famously said she stopped *wanting* success and started expecting alignment. She didn't wait for permission. She embodied abundance before the world confirmed it.

She didn't say:

"I want to be influential."

She lived as:

"I am a vessel for impact."

And the world rearranged.

Stop Asking "When and How" — That's Not Yor Job

Here's the truth nobody tells us:

👉 The "when" and the "how" are not required for manifestation or alignment.

Focusing on *when* creates impatience.
Focusing on *how* creates anxiety.
Both pull you out of the present moment—where your power actually lives.

Why "When" and "How" Block Flow

- "When will it happen?" = pressure
- "How will it work?" = control
- "Why hasn't it come yet?" = frustration

Your brain cannot create from stress.
Your heart cannot open from fear.

The Shift

Instead of asking:

- "When will love come?"

Ask: "How does the loved version of me live today?"
Instead of:

- "How will abundance find me?"

Ask: "How does an abundant woman move through her day?"
Alignment always responds to now.

Celebrity Example

Beyoncé didn't ask *when* Renaissance would be understood.
She created from identity, not timing.
She moved as:
"I am creative freedom."
The culture caught up later.

Visualization Is Not Daydreaming – It's Training

Visualization is not pretending.
It is rehearsal for the nervous system.

Your brain does not know the difference between:
• a vividly imagined experience
• and a lived one
When you visualize and feel, you teach your body what safety, joy, and abundance feel like.

How to Visualize Correctly
Not:

✕ "I hope this happens someday."
But:

✓ "This is how I feel when it exists."
Focus on:
• how your body feels
• how your breath moves
• how calm your nervous system becomes
• how grounded your heart feels
You're not visualizing *things*.
You're visualizing states of being.

Celebrity Example
Jim Carrey famously visualized success and *felt* gratitude long before it arrived.
He embodied certainty before evidence showed up.
He didn't wait to feel worthy.
He practiced feeling worthy.

Frequency – When Mind and Heart Agree
Abundance responds to coherence.
That means:
• Your thoughts (mind)
• Your emotions (heart)
• Your behaviors (body)
…are aligned.

You cannot think abundance while emotionally living in fear.
You cannot affirm love while bracing for disappointment.

Mind–Heart Alignment Looks Like

• Thinking: "I am safe."
• Feeling: calm instead of guarded
• Acting: choosing peace over chaos
This alignment sends a signal:
"I am ready."

Celebrity Example

Viola Davis has spoken openly about healing her inner narrative
before receiving the roles and love she desired. Her success
expanded when her *self-perception* healed.
Her frequency changed.
Her life followed.

Daily Practice – Reprogramming Into "I Am"

Step 1: Replace Wanting Language

Instead of:
• "I want peace."
Say:
• "I am choosing peace."
Instead of:
• "I want love."
Say:
• "I am open, worthy, and available for healthy love."

Step 2: Anchor in the Present

Ask daily:
• **"What does the aligned version of me do today?"**
Then do *that.*

Step 3: Feel Before You See
Before the thing arrives:
• feel gratitude
• feel calm
• feel safety
• feel joy
Feeling is the invitation.

Why This Works – The Soft Life Connection

Soft life is not about ease alone.
It's about internal safety.
When you move from:
• wanting → being
• chasing → allowing
• forcing → trusting
You exit survival mode.
And softness becomes possible.

The Day I Learned I Would Never Be Invisible Again

There is a moment in every woman's life when a quiet injustice
lights a fire she didn't yet know she possessed.
Mine happened when I was nineteen years old.
I was a sophomore at Temple University, working for a law firm
called Korn, Kline & Kutner—and yes, the irony of the acronym
KKK is not lost on me. I swear, I could not make this up if I tried.
I was young, ambitious, grateful to have a professional job, and
eager to learn. Every morning, one of the senior partners—Mr.
Kline—would walk into the office. Without fail. Like clockwork.
And every morning, he would walk directly past me.
He would greet my white colleague loudly and proudly.
"Good morning!"

"How are you?"
Big smile. Full acknowledgment.
And then… nothing.
No eye contact.
No greeting.
No nod.
No acknowledgment that I even existed.
At first, I told myself it was nothing.
I brushed it off.
I was young.
I needed my job.
I didn't want to "make waves."
But over time, the silence became loud.
It wasn't just uncomfortable for me—it became uncomfortable for
my colleague too. She noticed it. She felt it. The air in the room
would shift every morning when I was skipped over like I wasn't
there.
And still—I said nothing.
Because I was nineteen.
Because I was Black.
Because I needed the paycheck.
Because I didn't yet have the language, the confidence, or the
power to confront what I knew in my spirit was wrong.
But let me tell you what I *did* feel.
I felt invisible.
I felt small.
I felt less than.
I felt unworthy.
And even though I didn't speak up *then*, something else happened
instead.
I remembered.
I stored that feeling away—not as bitterness, but as fuel.
Because something inside me quietly decided that day:
I will never allow anyone to make me feel invisible again.

That moment became a catalyst.
It lit a fire I didn't yet know how to use—but it burned anyway.
That experience planted the seed for the woman I would become:
- The woman who speaks up.
- The woman who takes up space.
- The woman who does not shrink for comfort.
- The woman who demands respect without asking permission.
- The woman who walks into rooms knowing her presence matters.

That nineteen-year-old girl didn't confront the injustice out loud—but she confronted it internally. And that internal decision changed everything.
Because courage doesn't always show up as confrontation.
Sometimes it shows up as a vow to yourself.
A vow that says:
"Never again."
Never again will I tolerate disrespect.
Never again will I accept invisibility.
Never again will I question my worth because someone else refuses to see it.
That moment didn't break me.
It built me.
And every time I speak boldly today…
Every time I advocate fiercely…
Every time I walk in a room knowing I belong…
Every time I refuse to dim my light…
I honor that nineteen-year-old girl who learned—too early, but powerfully—that visibility is a form of self-respect.
That experience helped forge the courageous, outspoken, grounded woman I am today.
Not because I was angry.
But because I was awakened.

Life Is About Evolution — If You're Not Evolving, You're Just Existing

There is a truth I have lived by for as long as I can remember:

Life is about evolution.

If you're not evolving, you're just existing — not living.

And I didn't just say this to myself.

I poured it into my son.

From the time Jordan was about five years old, I repeated the same message over and over:

Keep growing.

Keep learning.

Keep exploring.

Try new things.

Stretch yourself.

I wanted him to understand early that comfort zones are dangerous places — because nothing grows there.

The one phrase I absolutely could not stand hearing from him was:

"I can't."

My response was always the same:

"How do you know you can't… if you haven't even tried?"

That wasn't harsh.

That was love.

That was leadership.

That was preparation for life.

Because fear disguises itself as "I can't."

And evolution begins the moment you challenge that lie.

The Moment I Knew He Was Listening

Like most parents, there were moments I wondered:

Is he really hearing me?

Is any of this sinking in?

Then one day, I opened Instagram.

I clicked on my son's profile.

Under his picture was my quote:
"Life is about evolving."
— *Mom*
I froze.
And then my heart melted.
A few years later, he took it even further.
Jordan got a tattoo.
Bold. Permanent. Intentional.
"EVOLVING."
Big letters.
Three years ago.
That's when it hit me:
Your words don't disappear.
They plant roots.
And when you live what you teach, your children — and everyone watching — carry it forward.

Why Evolution Is the Core of "I AM HER" Energy

Walking in *I AM HER* energy means you no longer fear reinvention.

HER understands:

- Growth will require discomfort
- Evolution will require shedding
- Expansion will require courage

But HER also knows:

Stagnation is spiritual suffocation.

You don't evolve because something is wrong with you.

You evolve because something is right with you.

HER doesn't cling to old identities.

HER doesn't romanticize outdated versions of herself.

HER doesn't say:

"This is just how I am."

HER says:
"This is who I am becoming."

Celebrity Examples: Women Who Chose Evolution Over Comfort

Beyoncé

She didn't stay in Destiny's Child.

She didn't stay in one sound.

She didn't stay in one image.

She evolved — artistically, spiritually, and personally.

Each era wasn't a reinvention for attention.

It was evolution rooted in truth.

Michelle Obama

She evolved from:

- working-class South Side Chicago
- to corporate attorney
- to First Lady
- to global author, speaker, and cultural architect

She has said openly:

"You're allowed to change your mind. You're allowed to grow."

That's evolution.

Oprah Winfrey

Oprah did not stay boxed into talk show host.

She evolved into a movement.

Media.

Education.

Spiritual leadership.

Ownership.

She followed expansion — not expectations.

Tracee Ellis Ross

She refuses to let age, marital status, or public pressure define her worth.

She evolves joyfully.

Loudly.

Softly.
On her own timeline.
That is *living*, not existing.

Evolution Requires Courage — Especially for Women
Let's be honest.
Women are often punished for evolving.
When you change:
- people get uncomfortable
- old versions of you feel entitled to access
- others accuse you of "switching up"
- some try to pull you back into familiarity

But HER understands:
Evolution threatens people who benefit from your stagnation.
You are not meant to stay who you were at:
- **25**
- **35**
- **45**
- or even last year

Growth is not betrayal.
Evolution is obedience to your becoming.

A Message to Every Woman Reading This

Sis, hear me clearly:
Never be afraid to:
- evolve
- explore
- reinvent yourself
- try something new
- leave what no longer fits
- dream bigger
- outgrow old versions of you

If you're still breathing, you're still becoming.

And if you've been feeling restless…
Unfulfilled…
Bored…
Tight…
Disconnected…
That's not failure.
That's evolution knocking.
Answer the door.

HER Knows This Truth
HER does not fear growth.
HER does not apologize for expansion.
HER does not shrink to stay familiar.
HER lives.
HER stretches.
HER tries.
HER evolves.
And when HER children — literal or spiritual — look back on her
life, they will say:
"She didn't just survive.
She lived."

Affirmation for This Section
"I give myself permission to evolve, expand, and become more.
I am not here to stay the same — I am here to LIVE."
— *Chanel Brooks*

SECTION TWO: The Era of HER

Every woman has a before HER life and an after HER life.
Before HER:
- she questioned her worth
- she accepted less than she deserved
- she over-explained, over-gave, over-apologized

- she lived in survival mode instead of intentional living

After HER:

- she knows who she is
- she stands on business and boundaries
- she embodies confidence without performing it
- she expects reciprocity, not excuses
- she chooses alignment, not attachment
- she walks in favor, not fear

From becoming HER to being HER— out loud, without hesitation, without guilt.

You've done the healing.

You've set the boundaries.

You've released the old.

You've embraced love.

You've rebuilt yourself.

Now it's time to embody the woman you have become.

Celebrity mirror:

This is what we watched happen with Beyoncé—not just "glowing up," but *owning herself* **at every level: artistry, privacy, motherhood, marriage, and power. HER energy isn't loud. It's undeniable.**

What "I AM HER" Energy Actually Means

Let's clarify this right now:

"I AM HER" is not arrogance.

It's not ego.

It's not superiority.

It's spiritual authority.

It's emotional maturity.

It's self-trust.

It's divine alignment.

"I AM HER" means:

1.   You trust your decisions.

You're not asking five people what you already know in your spirit.

2.   You walk into rooms like you belong there—because you do.

Not because you're better. Because you're *ready*.

3.   You speak softly and carry truth strongly.

You don't raise your voice to prove your point.

4.   Your boundaries are solid—but your heart stays open.

You don't become cold. You become clear.

5.   Your peace is your priority, not your leftover.

You don't earn rest. You honor it.

6.   You don't react—you respond.

And sometimes? Not responding is the response.

7.   You give gracefully and receive boldly.

No guilt for being supported.

8.   You celebrate yourself and clap for others without shrinking.

You can shine without competition.

9.   You know everything connected to you must rise with you.

Not because you're demanding—because you're discerning.

That's HER.

Celebrity mirror:

This is Angela Bassett energy. Decades of excellence, no begging for approval, no chasing relevance—just *presence*. She doesn't convince. She arrives.

---

he Difference Between Confidence and HER Confidence

There's regular confidence… and then there's embodied confidence.

Regular confidence can be shaken by:

- a rude comment
- a rejection

- someone's opinion
- a bad day

HER confidence is anchored.

HER confidence says: *"I don't need everything to go my way to know I'm still chosen."*

Celebrity mirror:

Rihanna is a case study in this. She doesn't over-explain her evolution—music, beauty, motherhood, fashion. She moves like someone who already knows: *"I am not here to be understood. I'm here to be myself."*

Signs You Have Stepped Into Your "HER" Era

When you're in your HER era, certain behaviors just… die.

✦ 1. You don't chase anymore.

Not relationships. Not job titles. Not validation. Not friendships. What is aligned comes to you.

✦ 2. You're comfortable saying, "This is not for me."

No guilt. No fuss. No dissertation.

✦ 3. You don't argue about who you are.

Your life is the evidence. Your peace is the proof.

✦ 4. You require effort, not potential.

Potential has never loved anybody right. Effort does.

✦ 5. You trust your healing, even on hard days.

A hard day doesn't mean you're back at the beginning.

✦ 6. Starting over doesn't scare you.

Because you finally trust you.

✦ 7. You attract friendships that feed you.

Not friendships that feed off you.

✦ 8. Chaos feels foreign now.

Drama sounds like a language you forgot.

✦ 9. You're living soft and strong at the same time.
Balanced. Whole. Deep. Aligned.
Celebrity mirror:
This is Michelle Obama in a sentence: boundaries, peace, purpose, no performative perfection—just grounded power.

How Black Women Lose "HER" (And How We Reclaim Her)

Let's talk about it for real.
We lose HER when we:
- carry too much
- overgive
- ignore our bodies
- silence intuition
- perform strength
- stay loyal to the wrong people
- accept crumbs and call it love
- fear being alone more than we fear being misaligned

But here's the truth:
Black women always find HER again.
We risc. We return. We reclaim.
HER is never gone—only buried under responsibility.
Celebrity mirror:
Taraji P. Henson speaking openly about mental health is HER energy. Because HER doesn't just "push through." HER tells the truth and chooses healing.

Real-Life Integration (Inspired by Me, Chanel)

I walk in HER energy when I:
- choose peace over people's opinions
- ask for what I deserve—and refuse what I don't

- love my husband Donoven with gratitude and maturity, not fear and performance
- lead with compassion but don't carry emotional dead weight
- travel, dress well, rest deeply, live boldly
- write this book and give other women language for their freedom

That's not a glow-up. That's a return.

The 7 Pillars of "I AM HER" Energy

If HER had a foundation, it would be these seven pillars:

✦ 1. HER Speaks With Authority

Not arrogance—authority.

HER doesn't soften truth to make people comfortable.

Celebrity mirror: Oprah—she doesn't argue. She states. She owns.

✦ 2. HER Walks With Divine Confidence

Divine confidence is quiet. It shifts the room without trying.

Celebrity mirror: Viola Davis—she owns space with truth, not theatrics.

✦ 3. HER Honors Her Feminine Power

Softness. Rest. Sensuality. Intuition. Joy. Vulnerability.

HER knows femininity isn't weakness—it's wisdom.

Celebrity mirror: Tabitha Brown—soft life energy as a ministry.

✦ 4. HER Protects Her Peace Like a Vault

HER doesn't debate boundaries. She enforces them.

Celebrity mirror: Serena Williams stepping away and evolving—choosing life alignment over public demands.

✦ 5. HER Chooses Alignment Over Approval

HER does not live to be liked.

HER lives to be lit from within.

Celebrity mirror: Tracee Ellis Ross—unapologetic about standards and joy.

6. HER Invests in Herself

Time. Therapy. Wellness. Beauty. Education. Rest.

HER reinvests in herself because she is her greatest asset.

Celebrity mirror: Mary J. Blige in her "Good Morning Gorgeous" era—self-love made visible.

7. HER Lives Like Her Dreams Belong to Her

HER doesn't ask "Why me?"

HER asks "Why not me?"

Celebrity mirror: Beyoncé—ownership, vision, precision, and ease.

How to Maintain Your "I AM HER" Energy

Becoming HER was the journey.

Staying HER is the practice.

STEP 1: Protect Your Nervous System

If your peace is disturbed, your power gets compromised.

Monitor:

- who gets access
- what environments feed you
- what conversations drain you
- what habits spike your stress

Peace is a boundary, not a bonus.

STEP 2: Speak HER Language Daily

Say it out loud:

- "I am chosen."
- "I am worthy."
- "I am aligned."
- "I am soft and supported."
- "I am protected."
- "I am becoming my own answered prayer."
- "I AM HER."

STEP 3: Live in Intentional Excellence
HER doesn't rush.
HER doesn't beg.
HER doesn't settle.
HER moves like God and her ancestors are on her planning committee.
STEP 4: Keep Your Circle Clean
Your elevation requires:
- supporters
- expanders
- encouragers

Not critics, drains, and jealous spirits.
STEP 5: Make Choices Your Future Self Will Thank You For
Ask: "What does HER choose today?"
Then do that.

Section Eight: The "HER" Reset for Hard Days

Because yes—HER has hard days too.
On hard days, HER does three things:
1.   She returns to her body.
Water. Walk. Stretch. Breath. Sleep. Food.
Because emotional regulation is spiritual maintenance.
2.   She returns to truth.
"What do I know for sure?"
Not what I fear. Not what I assume. Truth.
3.   She returns to boundaries.
Hard days require less access, not more chaos.
Celebrity mirror:
Even Simone Biles choosing her mental wellness was HER energy.
It wasn't quitting. It was sovereignty.

Homework — The Embodied HER Assignment

Homework #1: Write Your HER Declaration

Start with: "I am the woman who…"

Make it one strong paragraph.

Homework #2: Dress Like HER for One Full Week

Not for attention—for identity reinforcement.

Homework #3: Create a "No Longer" List

What HER no longer:

- accepts
- tolerates
- entertains
- explains
- participates in

Homework #4: Allow Yourself to Be Seen

Post a picture.

Share a win.

Tell the truth.

HER doesn't hide her light.

Homework #5: 21-Day Morning Mantra

Say this every morning:

"I am HER—fully, boldly, and beautifully. I walk in my power and honor the woman I have become."

Exercise: Meet the HER Version of You

Write a one-page letter titled: "A Day in the Life of HER."

Describe:

- how she wakes up
- what she believes
- how she speaks
- what she wears
- what she refuses
- what she allows

- who has access
- what peace looks like
- what love feels like
- what she does when life tries her

This becomes your blueprint.

Final Affirmation for Chapter Nine

"You don't become HER by wishing—you become HER by walking. Every decision, every boundary, every yes, every no builds the woman you were destined to be." – *Chanel Brooks*

I AM HER WORKSHEET

From Identity to Embodiment

Purpose:

This worksheet helps you shift from *wanting* to *being* by grounding your nervous system, clarifying your identity, and locking in your "I AM HER" energy.

Take your time. Write slowly. Answer honestly. This is not about perfection — it's about presence.

SECTION 1: WHO IS "HER" FOR YOU?

Complete the sentence below without censoring yourself:

HER is the woman who…

____

____

____

Now describe her in detail:

- How does she carry herself?

- How does she speak to herself when things go wrong?

- What does she no longer tolerate?

- What does she expect as normal?

Section Two: From "I Want" to "I Am" (Identity Shift)

Rewrite each statement from *wanting* into *being*.

I WANT…	I AM…
I want peace	I am choosing peace daily
I want love	_________________________
I want abundance	_________________________

I WANT...   I AM...

I want confidence _______________________________________

I want ease   _______________________________________

Now write 3 original "I AM" statements that describe who you are becoming right now:

1.   I am

____

2.   I am

____

3.   I am

____

Section Three: What Does Her Feel Like In Her Body?

Close your eyes for 30 seconds. Breathe deeply. Then answer:

•   When HER walks into a room, her body feels:

☐ Calm   ☐ Grounded   ☐ Open   ☐ Relaxed   ☐ Safe

•   HER nervous system feels:

____

•   HER breath feels:

☐ Slow   ☐ Steady   ☐ Deep   ☐ Free

•   HER heart feels:

____

This is your frequency. Memorize it. Return to it often.

Section Four: Her Daily Chpices

Answer honestly:

1.   One thing HER says **NO** to without guilt:

____

2.   One thing HER says **YES** to with intention:

____

3.   One habit HER is releasing:

____

4.   One habit HER is committing to:

171

Section Five: Her Standards (Non-Negotiables)
HER does not negotiate on:

- Peace:

____

- Respect:

____

- Love:

____

- Energy:

____

Write this sentence and finish it:
"Anything that disrupts my ___________ is no longer allowed access to me."

Section Six: Her Circle & Access
List the types of people HER allows close:

✓

____

✓

____

✓

____

List what HER no longer entertains:

✗

____

✗

____

✗

____

Section Seven: Her Visualization Practice:
Complete this slowly:
A day in HER life feels like…
• Morning energy:

____

• Daily rhythm:

____

• Emotional state:

____

• Evening peace:

____

Read this visualization once a day for the next 7 days.

Section Eight: The HER Declaration
Write your declaration in your own words:
I am the woman who…

____

____

____

____

Sign your name below as a commitment to yourself:
Signed: _______________________________
Date: _______________________________

DAILY "I AM HER" AFFIRMATION
Say this out loud every morning:
"I am grounded. I am aligned. I am safe to receive.
I trust myself. I trust my timing.
I walk in my power with softness and certainty.
I AM HER."

How to Use This Worksheet

✔ Complete once, revisit weekly

✔ Pair with journaling or meditation

✔ Use before major decisions

✔ Keep near your bed or mirror

Chapter Ten
THE SOFT LIFE YOU DESERVE
(Because Your Healing Journey Deserves a Joyful Destination)

INTRODUCTION: LETTING GO OF SURVIVAL MODE WHEN YOU FINALLY FEEL SAFE

When the Armor Comes Off and the Soft Life Begins

One of the most overlooked parts of healing is this:

Learning how to rest once survival is no longer required.

When I first met my husband, Donoven, loving him wasn't the hard part.

Letting go of survival mode was.

For over a decade, it was just me.
I carried everything.
I managed everything.
I planned everything.
I paid everything.
I protected everything.
My son was my priority.
My household was my responsibility.
My life required constant vigilance.
There was no backup plan.
No safety net.
No margin for error.
Survival mode wasn't a mindset — it was a necessity.
And when you live like that long enough, it doesn't turn off
automatically just because love shows up.

SURVIVAL MODE *vs.* SOFT LIFE

Survival Doesn't Have to Be a Lifestyle. **Lean Into Softness.**

SURVIVAL MODE	SOFT LIFE
Hyper-Independence	Rest in Partnership
Anxious Hustle	Graceful Flow
Constant Defense	Protected Peace
Overworking to Cope	Balance of Love & Ambition
Chronic Overwhelm	Emotional Regulation
Guarded Heart	Softened Heart
"I Got It" Energy	"I Receive" Energy
Living Tense, Tired, And Alone	Living Nourished, Balanced, And Loved.

Survival Mode Says,
"I'm the only one who has me."

Soft Life Says,
"I can exhale because I'm supported."

THE SHIFT: From SURVIVING to THRIVING

Survival Mode Says,
"I'm the only one who has me."

Soft Life Says,
"I can exhale because I'm supported."

From Hustle to Harmony

Sis, you've done the work.

You healed the wounds you used to pretend didn't hurt.

You set boundaries you used to feel guilty about.

You stopped chasing what was never yours.

You learned how to love yourself loudly.

You became the woman you prayed for.

Now comes the part nobody prepares you for: receiving.

Because the soft life isn't just the reward.

It's the destination—the place your healing was trying to take you all along.

Not softness as weakness.

Softness as freedom.

Softness as safety.

Softness as a nervous system that finally gets to unclench.

Celebrity mirror:

When Michelle Obama stepped into life after the White House, she modeled something powerful: purpose *without* punishment. Joy *without* explanation. Boundaries *without* apology. That's soft life energy—still impactful, just not depleted.

Section One: What Is the Soft Life, Really?

Let's clear the air: soft life is not laziness.

It's not "I do nothing all day."

It's not aesthetic-only—robes, candles, and a caption.

Soft life is an internal shift that changes your external reality.

Soft life means:

- choosing rest over burnout
- enjoying joy without guilt
- allowing luxury (however *you* define luxury)
- creating space for beauty, pleasure, and peace
- releasing the belief that you must suffer to be worthy
- living in alignment instead of constant resistance

Soft life is not about having a perfect life.

It's about having a peaceful relationship with your life.

Celebrity mirror:

Tabitha Brown is a living example of soft life as a spiritual practice. She moves gently, speaks kindly, protects her peace, and still builds an empire—without chaos as the fuel.

Section Two: How We Were Conditioned to Think Softness Is Unsafe

For many women—especially Black women—softness was treated like a luxury we didn't have time for.

We were raised to be:

- the backbone
- the fixer
- the "strong one"
- the dependable one
- the emotional anchor
- the one who "handles it"

But if you're everybody's backbone… who holds you?

Soft life requires unlearning:

- that rest must be earned
- that asking for help makes you needy
- that struggle is noble
- that "busy" equals valuable
- that peace is selfish
- that softness makes you less respected

Sis… soft life is not a reward for being perfect.

It's your birthright as a whole woman.

Celebrity mirror:

When Taraji P. Henson speaks openly about mental health, she's challenging the "strong woman who never breaks" lie. Soft life starts when you stop pretending you're fine.

Section Three: Why You Deserve the Soft Life (Yes, You)

You deserve the soft life because you've spent enough years in hard seasons.

You deserve it because:

- you've done the inner work
- you've carried responsibilities others never saw
- you've shown up through grief, pressure, and disappointment
- you've been the answer for everyone else
- you've survived things you shouldn't have had to survive

And here's the bigger truth:

Rest is revolutionary.

In a world that profits off your exhaustion, softness is a quiet rebellion.

Celebrity mirror:

Ariana Grande stepping back when life demanded gentleness, and Simone Biles choosing mental wellness—both show the same message: "My peace matters more than performance."

Section Four: Soft Life Isn't Aesthetic—It's Nervous System Safety

People think soft life looks like:

- vacations
- spa days
- silk pajamas
- brunch
- candles

Cute. But the real soft life is internal.

Soft life is:

- not waking up anxious every morning
- not living on edge waiting for the next crisis

- not being addicted to chaos
- not accepting love that hurts
- not keeping access open to people who drain you
- not sacrificing yourself to prove you're "good"

Soft life is emotional wealth.

Calm. Centered. Supported. Safe. Present.

Ask yourself:

Do I feel safe in my own life?

If the answer is "not really," the soft life isn't optional. It's necessary.

Section Five: The 10 Pillars of a Soft Life

Here's the blueprint. No confusion.

1) Peace Is the Priority

If it disturbs your peace, it gets evaluated—fast.

2) Rest Without Apology

You don't earn rest by suffering first. You rest because you're human.

3) Boundaries Are Love

Softness requires limits. Period.

4) Receiving Is a Skill

Compliments. Help. Support. Love. Gifts.

Say "thank you" and let it land.

5) "No" Is a Complete Sentence

No long explanation. No guilt. No overthinking.

6) Joy Is Scheduled

Not "if I have time." Joy goes on the calendar.

7) Your Home Becomes a Sanctuary

Your environment should feel like an exhale.

8) Your Relationships Feel Safe

You can breathe around the people you love—no walking on eggshells.

9) Your Body Is Treated With Gentleness

Nourishment. Movement. Sleep. Hydration. Care.

You stop punishing your body for surviving.

10) You Live Slower on Purpose

Soft life is presence.

Feeling your life instead of racing through it.

Celebrity mirror:

Meghan Markle choosing peace over performance is a pillar example: "I'm not sacrificing my wellbeing to keep up an image."

Section Six: What Soft Life Requires You to Release

You can't live softly while gripping hard things.

Soft life requires releasing:

- guilt around rest
- people-pleasing
- survival relationships
- overfunctioning
- perfectionism
- "I'll be happy when…" thinking
- loyalty to patterns that keep you drained
- the belief that you must do everything alone

Soft life is not about becoming less ambitious.

It's about becoming less available for suffering.

Section Seven: Soft Life in Love—When Peace Becomes the Standard

A soft life requires love that doesn't trigger survival mode.

Healthy love looks like:

- clarity
- consistency
- emotional safety

- laughter
- partnership
- someone who carries weight *with* you

My marriage to Donoven is a soft life multiplier because it reflects what healed love does:

it lets your nervous system relax.

It lets you exhale.

It makes space for softness without fear.

Celebrity mirror:

Ciara has spoken about choosing herself, healing, and then attracting a love that matched her standards. That's soft life love—peaceful, grown, aligned.

Section Eight: Real-Life Integration (Inspired by Me, Chanel)

Soft life doesn't mean I stop being powerful.

It means I stop being punished by my power.

My soft life looks like:

- working with purpose and still protecting my weekends
- choosing luxury experiences without waiting for permission
- traveling and enjoying life without guilt
- saying no to the fixer role
- resting like it's holy—because it is
- loving in a way that feels safe
- writing my story and still taking my time with myself

This is the healed woman's flex: peace that doesn't require explanation.

Section Nine: Soft Life Practices You Can Start This Week

Here are practical ways to step into softness right now:

1) The "Two Yeses" Rule

Before you agree to anything, ask:

- Is this a yes for my spirit?
- Is this a yes for my schedule?

If you can't answer yes to both, pause.

2) One Gentle Hour a Day

One hour with no fixing, no rescuing, no productivity pressure.

Just being.

3) Replace One Hard Habit

- scrolling → reading
- chaos friends → peaceful friends
- overworking → delegation
- neglecting body → nourishment

4) Build a Soft Morning

Your first 20 minutes set the tone:

water, prayer, quiet, stretch, music, gratitude.

5) Weekly Beauty Ritual

Flowers. Nails. Massage. Long shower. A date with yourself.

Not as a reward—as maintenance.

Section Ten: Exercises and Reflection

Soft Life Inventory

Answer honestly:

1. Where am I still operating in survival mode?
2. What drains me most consistently?
3. Where do I need support but refuse to ask?
4. What relationship feels rough instead of soft?
5. What would my life look like if I lived gently on purpose?

Reflection Prompt: Design Your Soft Life

Write one full page starting with:

"My soft life looks like…"

Include:

- how you wake up
- what your home feels like

- how love shows up
- how you handle stress
- what peace costs (and what you're willing to pay)
- what you no longer tolerate

This becomes your map.

FINAL AFFIRMATION FOR CHAPTER TEN

"The soft life isn't a luxury. It's the reward for every battle you survived, every lesson you learned, and every version of you that had to die so your peace could finally live." — ***Chanel Brooks***

FINAL CHAPTER
She Rises: Stepping Into the Rest of Your Life
(Where Survival Ends and Sovereignty Begins)

INTRODUCTION: THIS IS NOT THE END – THIS IS YOUR ARRIVAL

Sis… pause for a moment.

If you're holding this book in your hands, it means you didn't just *read* it — you *walked through it.*

You confronted truth.

You sat with discomfort.

You released what no longer fit.

You remembered who you are.

This chapter is not a conclusion.

It's a coronation.

Because somewhere between slowing the hell down, losing the luggage, burying old identities, loving yourself loudly, becoming

HER, choosing softness, and learning to evolve instead of endure
— something irreversible happened:
You rose.
Not loudly.
Not dramatically.
But decisively.
This is the chapter where you stop surviving your life
and start stewarding it.

Section One: You Are No Longer the Woman Who Needed This Book — You Are the Woman Who LIVED It

Let's name this clearly.
You are not the woman who:

- tolerated crumbs and called it loyalty
- confused chaos with chemistry
- stayed too long because leaving felt scary
- carried everything alone and called it strength
- lived in survival mode disguised as productivity
- waited for permission to choose herself

That woman served her purpose.
She protected you when you didn't know how.
She helped you survive what tried to break you.
But she does not get to lead your future.
The woman closing this book is:

- discerning
- grounded
- self-led
- emotionally mature
- soft without being weak
- powerful without being loud
- open without being naïve
- healed enough to receive

- wise enough to walk away
- aligned enough to wait
- brave enough to live

That woman is HER.
And HER doesn't just rise —
she stays risen.

Section Two: When Survival Ends, Sovereignty Begins

Survival taught you how to *endure*.
Sovereignty teaches you how to *choose*.
Survival says:
"Just get through it."
Sovereignty says:
"This no longer aligns with who I am."
Survival says:
"I'll figure it out myself."
Sovereignty says:
"I am allowed support, rest, and reciprocity."
Survival says:
"I can't stop now."
Sovereignty says:
"I don't need to rush what's already meant for me."
This is the moment where you stop asking:

- *What will they think?*
- *What if this doesn't work?*
- *What if I'm wrong?*

And start asking:

- *Does this honor my peace?*
- *Does this reflect my growth?*
- *Does this feel like home to my spirit?*

That shift is not small.
That shift is everything.

Section Three: The Women Who Rose — And Stayed There

History is filled with women who didn't peak early —
they arrived late, deeper, and stronger.
Viola Davis didn't become a household name until her forties —
after rejection, poverty, and invisibility. When she rose, she didn't
shrink. She brought her whole story with her.
Oprah Winfrey didn't "win" because she was perfect — she won
because she became aligned. She stopped performing survival and
started living truth.
Michelle Obama showed the world that power doesn't need
volume. Her rise came through clarity, boundaries, and self-respect.
Mary J. Blige didn't find her voice when she was broken — she
found it when she chose herself. *Good Morning Gorgeous* wasn't an
album. It was a declaration.
These women didn't rush their becoming.
They honored the process.
They did the work.
And when they rose — they didn't go back.
Neither will you.

Section Four: What It Means to Rise — For Real

Rising doesn't mean life gets perfect.
It means you stop abandoning yourself when life gets hard.
Rising means:

- you digest instead of suppress
- you accept instead of resist
- you move instead of stay stuck
- you note-take so lessons don't repeat

Rising means:

- you no longer stay where you're tolerated
- you no longer audition for love
- you no longer make men, jobs, or friendships your science projects
- you no longer allow others to define your narrative

Rising means:
- you trust your timing
- you trust your discernment
- you trust your evolution

Rising means:
- you don't chase alignment — you *attract* it
- you don't beg for peace — you *protect* it
- you don't ask if it's too late — you *move anyway*

Rising means:

You live.

Fully.

Softly.

Boldly.

Intentionally.

Section Five: The Rest of Your Life Is Not a Mystery — It's a Choice

Here is the truth no one told us early enough:

The rest of your life doesn't begin when everything is figured out.

It begins when you decide to live as the woman you've become.

You don't need:
- a perfect plan
- universal approval
- permission from the past
- validation from people who benefited from the old you

You need alignment.

You need courage.

You need trust.

The woman you are now knows how to:

- walk away without guilt
- stay still without fear
- love without losing herself
- lead without performing
- rest without explaining
- receive without shrinking

This is not the life you *dreamed* about.

This is the life you prepared for.

Section Six: A Promise to Yourself — The HER Covenant

Before you close this book, make this promise:

I promise to never return to survival

when peace is available.

I promise to never dim my light

to keep others comfortable.

I promise to evolve — even when it's inconvenient.

I promise to choose softness

without surrendering strength.

I promise to honor my body, my spirit, my time, and my joy.

I promise to live — not just exist.

I promise to be HER

even when it's easier to be familiar.

This is not a vow to perfection.

It is a vow to presence.

FINAL BLESSING: From Me to You

Sis…

You didn't miss your moment.

You didn't start too late.

You didn't wait too long.

You are not behind.

You were becoming.
And now?
You rise.
Not to prove anything.
Not to perform healing.
Not to impress the world.
You rise because you are ready to live the rest of your life
with intention, alignment, softness, and power.
Close this book knowing this:
You are not lost.
You are not broken.
You are not unfinished.
You are HER.
Fully.
Finally.
And forever.

FINAL QUOTE OF THE BOOK
"There is no greater revolution than a woman who survives her past, honors her present, and rises into the rest of her life unapologetically."
— *Chanel B. Brooks*

BOOK DISCUSSION & REFLECTION GUIDE

If "Slow the Hell Down" Was a Person: The Case of the Missing Luggage
By Chanel B. Brooks

HOW TO USE THIS GUIDE
This guide is designed to:
- Encourage honest reflection
- Spark meaningful group conversation
- Help readers apply the lessons to real life
- Support emotional healing and personal evolution

Each section includes:
- Key Themes
- Discussion Questions
- Personal Reflection Prompts
- Application Exercises

Participants are encouraged to journal their responses and share only what feels safe.

SECTION 1: THE CASE OF THE MISSING LUGGAGE
Identity, Loss, and Self-Awareness
Key Themes
• Identity loss
• Emotional baggage
• Survival vs. self-awareness
• Naming what we carry
• The moment of awakening
Discussion Questions
1.	What does "missing luggage" symbolize in your own life?
2.	What parts of yourself have you lost, buried, or forgotten while surviving?

3.   When was the first moment you realized something in your life no longer fit?

4.   How does naming what you carry change how you move forward?

5.   Why do women often minimize emotional loss compared to physical loss?

Reflection Prompt

• What emotional luggage have I been carrying that I never chose intentionally?

Exercise

Write a list titled "What I've Been Carrying."

Circle the items that no longer belong in your next season.

SECTION 2: SLOW THE HELL DOWN — THE D.A.M.N. METHOD

Digest. Accept. Move. Note-Take. Now.

Key Themes

• Emotional regulation

• Conscious response

• Healing through awareness

• Growth through reflection

• Releasing reactivity

Discussion Questions

1.   Which part of the D.A.M.N. Method is hardest for you—and why?

2.   How does slowing down disrupt survival mode?

3.   What happens when we skip the "Digest" or "Accept" steps?

4.   How does Note-Taking turn pain into wisdom?

5.   How could this method change how you handle conflict, loss, or disappointment?

Reflection Prompt

• Where in my life am I rushing past lessons instead of learning from them?

Exercise

Apply the D.A.M.N. Method to a recent difficult situation. Write one sentence for each step.

SECTION 3: STOP FIGHTING BATTLES THAT AREN'T YOURS

Closure, Grief and Transformation

Key Themes

• Letting go of expired identities

• Grieving old versions of self

• Emotional closure

• Healing rituals

• Permission to move on

Discussion Questions

1.   What version of yourself have you outgrown but never properly released?

2.   Why do we resist grieving non-physical losses?

3.   How does unresolved grief show up in behavior?

4.   What would change if you honored your endings?

5.   How does grief create space for rebirth?

Reflection Prompt

• What do I need to lay to rest so I can fully live?

Exercise

Write a short "eulogy" for a version of yourself you've outgrown.

SECTION 4: NO IS A COMPLETE SENTENCE

Boundaries, Self-Respect, and Honoring Your Peace

Key Themes

•   boundaries

•   self-respect

•   letting go of guilt

•   honoring personal needs

•   protecting peace

Discussion Questions

1. Why do many people struggle with saying no?
2. What situations in your life require stronger boundaries?
3. How might your life change if you felt comfortable saying no without explanation?
4. What fears arise when you consider setting firmer boundaries?

Reflection Prompt

• Write down three situations where you feel pressured to say "yes" even when it does not serve your well-being.

Exercise

Next to each situation, write a boundary statement you could use instead.

Example:

"I appreciate the opportunity, but I'm not able to take that on right now."

Remember:

Setting boundaries is not rejection—it is self-respect.

SECTION 5: THE REBIRTH OF YOUR IDENTITY

Who You Were, Who You Became, Who You're Becoming

Key Themes

• Identity evolution
• Reinvention
• Self-definition
• Growth seasons
• Authentic living

Discussion Questions

1. Who were you before survival shaped you?
2. What identities were imposed on you?
3. How has your definition of success changed?
4. What does your next version require from you?
5. Who benefits when you stay small?

Reflection Prompt
• Who am I becoming—and what must change to support her?
Exercise
Create three columns: Past Me | Present Me | Becoming Me
Write five traits in each.

SECTION 6: LOVING YOURSELF LOUDLY
Visibility, Worth, and Self-Advocacy
Key Themes
• Self-worth
• Visibility
• Boundaries
• Confidence without apology
• Receiving love
Discussion Questions
1.   What does loving yourself loudly look like in practice?
2.   Why are women taught to love quietly?
3.   Where do you dim yourself for comfort?
4.   How does self-love change your relationships?
5.   What fears surface when you choose yourself?
Reflection Prompt
• Where am I still asking for permission to be seen?
Exercise
Write five ways you will love yourself more visibly this month.

SECTION 7: NEVER STAY WHERE YOU'RE ONLY TOLERATED
Tolerance vs. Appreciation | Placeholder vs. Partner
Key Themes
• Self-respect
• Boundaries
• Emotional availability

• Partnership vs. convenience
• Knowing when to walk away
Discussion Questions
1.   How do you define being "tolerated" versus "celebrated"?
2.   Where have you accepted placeholder treatment?
3.   Why do women stay in spaces where they are not chosen?
4.   What does partnership require that placeholders never receive?
5.   How does self-development shift how others treat you?
Reflection Prompt
• Where am I settling for proximity instead of partnership?
Exercise
List three non-negotiables you now require to stay in any relationship.

SECTION 8: BECOMING THE WOMAN YOU PRAYED FOR
Readiness, Alignment, and Love
Key Themes
• Emotional maturity
• Divine timing
• Self-preparation
• Healthy partnership
• Receiving love
Discussion Questions
1.   How does becoming precede receiving?
2.   What inner work prepared you for healthier love?
3.   Why does love arrive when we stop chasing?
4.   How does readiness differ from desire?
5.   What does aligned love feel like in the body?
Reflection Prompt

• What version of me is capable of sustaining the love I desire?

Exercise

Write a paragraph titled: "The Woman I Am Becoming for Love."

SECTION 9: WALKING IN YOUR "I AM HER" ENERGY

Embodiment, Confidence, and Peace

Key Themes

• Identity embodiment

• Authority

• Peace

• Confidence

• Alignment

Discussion Questions

1. What does "I AM HER" mean to you personally?
2. How does embodiment differ from aspiration?
3. Where do you still second-guess yourself?
4. What behaviors contradict your highest self?
5. How does peace signal alignment?

Reflection Prompt

• What would change if I trusted myself fully?

Exercise

Write a one-page HER Declaration beginning with:
"I am the woman who..."

SECTION 10: THE SOFT LIFE YOU DESERVE

Ease, Joy, and Abundance

Key Themes

• Rest

• Softness

• Nervous system safety

• Joy

• Receiving

Discussion Questions

1. How were you conditioned to equate struggle with worth?
2. What does softness look like beyond aesthetics?
3. Where are you still operating in survival mode?
4. How does peace change your decision-making?
5. What would it mean to live gently on purpose?

Reflection Prompt

• What would my life feel like if ease were my baseline?

Exercise

Design your Soft Life Blueprint (daily, weekly, relational).

FINAL SECTION: SHE RISES — STEPPING INTO THE REST OF YOUR LIFE

Integration, Sovereignty, and Forward Motion

Key Themes

• Integration
• Sovereignty
• Self-authorship
• Legacy
• Purpose

Discussion Questions

1. How has your definition of strength evolved?
2. What does sovereignty mean in your life now?
3. What chapter are you closing as you finish this book?
4. How will you protect what you've healed?
5. What promise are you making to yourself moving forward?

Reflection Prompt

• Who am I choosing to be from this moment forward?

Exercise

Write your HER Manifesto beginning with:
"From this day forward, I choose..."

About the Author

Chanel B. Brooks is a government affairs professional, registered lobbyist, transformational speaker, and advocate for women reclaiming their time, voice, and personal power.

With nearly three decades of professional experience in lobbying, community engagement, and organizational development, Chanel has built a career centered on empowering others to move forward with clarity, confidence, and purpose.

Chanel is also a registered lobbyist and seasoned government affairs professional who has spent her career building meaningful relationships between communities, organizations, and public leaders.

Through her writing and speaking, Chanel encourages women to pause, reflect, and reconnect with the version of themselves they may have lost while carrying the weight of expectations, responsibilities, and constant demands.

Her message is simple but powerful: slowing down is not weakness—it is wisdom.

If You Need to Slow the Hell Down Was a Person: The Case of the Missing Luggage is Chanel's invitation for readers to reclaim their peace, establish healthier boundaries, and embrace the life they truly deserve.

Chanel frequently speaks on topics including personal transformation, self-advocacy, lobbying and civic engagement, and the importance of creating space for rest, reflection, and renewal in a fast-paced world.

To learn more about Chanel's work, speaking engagements, and upcoming events, visit:

www.chanelbbrooks.com

Bring Chanel to Speak

If the message in this book resonated with you, imagine the power of experiencing it live.

Chanel B. Brooks is a dynamic speaker who inspires audiences to move beyond burnout, reclaim their personal power, and embrace lives rooted in purpose, balance, and confidence.

Through engaging storytelling, practical insight, and empowering strategies, Chanel helps women and organizations transform the way they approach leadership, boundaries, and personal well-being.

Chanel speaks on topics including:

- **From Survival Mode to Soft Life™**
- **The Power of Boundaries: Why "No" Is a Complete Sentence**
- **Reclaiming Your Time, Energy, and Identity**
- **Becoming the Woman You Were Meant to Be**
- **Leadership, Confidence, and Personal Transformation**

Her talks are ideal for:

- Women's conferences
- Corporate leadership events
- Churches and faith-based gatherings
- Professional development seminars
- Book clubs and community organizations

To inquire about booking **Chanel B. Brooks** for a speaking engagement, workshop, or panel discussion, please visit:

www.chanelbbrooks.com

Or email:

book@chanelbbrooks.com

A Quick Favor Before You Go

If this book spoke to you, encouraged you, or helped you see yourself in a new light, I have a small favor to ask.

Would you consider leaving a brief review on Amazon?

Reviews help other readers discover books that can inspire, encourage, and empower them during their own journeys. Even a few sentences about what resonated with you can make a meaningful difference.

Your voice helps this message reach the women who may need it most.

To leave a review, simply visit the book's page on Amazon and share your thoughts.

Thank you for taking this journey with me.

And remember:

Slowing down isn't giving up.

It's reclaiming your life.

With gratitude,

Chanel B. Brooks

Learn more at

www.chanelbbrooks.com